GRILL BOOK

GRILL BOOK

TEXT BY
KELLY MCCUNE

DESIGN BY
THOMAS INGALLS

PRODUCED BY
DAVID BARICH

HarperPerennial

A Division of HarperCollins*Publishers*

To Rob Miller, Patsy Barich, Gail Grant and Gordon McCune for their inspiration, advice and support; Russ "R. B." Barich, Ed and Mary Ingalls for teaching their sons to grill.

ACKNOWLEDGEMENTS

Thanks goes to Pagano's Hardware, Alameda, California; Star Route Farms, Bolinas, California; Courtyard Antiques and Interiors, Pearl's Oyster Bar and Stanford Florists, Palo Alto, California; Thomas Fogarty Winery, Portola Valley, California; La Ville Du Soleil, Lazzari Fuel Co., Inc. and Rush Cutters, San Francisco; and Mikasa, Secaucus, New Jersey.

Special thanks to Gordon Wing, Todd L. Koons, Andrew R. Forrest and Greg Stahl.

Thanks to Amy Nathan for her tasteful ideas and to a magic place called Chef Camp.where the idea for this book caught fire.

Quotation on page 5 from *A Sand County Almanac and Sketches Here and There* by Aldo Leopold. Copyright 1949, 1977 by Oxford University Press, Inc. Reprinted by permission.

For information address
HarperCollins Publishers Inc.
10 East 53rd Street
New York, NY 10022

Printed in Hong Kong.

Book and Cover Design:
Thomas Ingalls + Associates
Photography and Set Design:
Viktor Budnik
Food Styling and Props:
Karen Hazarian
Assistant to Photography:
Sandi Frank Stahl
Support: Dianne McKenzie

LIBRARY OF CONGRESS CATALOGING-IN-PUBLICATION DATA

McCune, Kelly.

   Includes index.
   1. Barbecue cookery. I. Ingalls, Thomas M. II. Barich, David. III. Title.
TX840.B3M43   1986
641.5'784   85-45213
ISBN 0-06-096006-X

92 93 94 95 15 14 13 12 11 10 9 8

We had cooked with white-oak coals in the corn belt, we had smudged our pots with pine in the north woods, we had browned vénison ribs over Arizona juniper, but we had not seen perfection until we roasted a young goose with Delta mesquite.

ALDO LEOPOLD
A Sand County Almanac

CONTENTS

FOREWORD

OCCASIONALLY one comes across a cookbook which so excites the palate that one wants to immediately run to the stove or in this case the grill. This is such a book: the gorgeous photographs, the clean design, and the clear and imaginative recipes make for an unbeatable combination.

I also love the use, throughout the book, of Asian ingredients, techniques and condiments: this East/West slant gives additional flavor to an already exciting volume. The author succeeds in giving essential information without ever belaboring the point and the recipes themselves are an eclectic blend of the familiar and the new.

In the end though, the true test of a useful cookbook is its ability to combine ease in use with tempting recipes and ideas, while conveying the sensuousness and fun that are at the heart of good food. I think that you will find, as I have, that the *Grill Book* meets the test. It epitomizes what grilling is about: food that's uncomplicated and delicious at the same time.

KEN HOM
Berkeley, California
November, 1985

INTRODUCTION

THE EARLIEST GRILLS

The ancient technique of cooking food over fire was first mastered well over 100,000 years ago. Early man discovered that he could roast meat over hot embers on long sticks, or place vegetables and fish wrapped in damp seaweed to cook on hot fire-pit stones. Over the long centuries man developed more sophisticated ways of cooking food using clay ovens, hearths, and stoves.

Our technique of cooking food on a grill – which we now variously call grilling, barbecuing, and charcoaling – was brought to America from a tiny island called Hispaniola in the Caribbean. During the seventeenth century, Hispaniola was a place of refuge for hundreds of shipwrecked sailors, runaway servants, and freebooters. These vagabonds learned the native Carib Indians' method of smoke-drying meat over hot coals on woven green wood grids. The Spanish were particularly fascinated by this new cooking tool, which they called a *barbacoa*. They carried the novelty with them into Mexico and the American Southwest, where it very quickly caught on. By the 1880s, cattle ranchers out on the range were using a metal version of the *barbacoa* to cook slabs of ribs and large hunks of meat to feed hungry cowboys. Eventually even the town folks began asking for their share of this new flavor sensation called "barbecue."

THE NEW AMERICAN GRILL

For decades the barbecue in America was an institution at large-scale social gatherings, and the numbers that turned out for these events confirmed its immense popularity. Politicians, fair organizers, and town social coordinators could be guaranteed large crowds if they promised "Texas-style" ribs, spit-roasted pig, or even barbecued turtles (an early New York specialty). One political rally *and* clambake in 1840 for presidential candidate William Henry Harrison drew over ten thousand people.

The post-war forties and fifties was a time of dramatic change in the American lifestyle. The country prospered, and people began moving to the more spacious suburbs, where they had garages, patios, and the newest luxury, *backyards*. Entertaining in these new backyards was a way of showing off, and what better way was there to attract folks than the ever popular barbecue? The first scaled-down home grill appeared around 1946, and the newest American summer pastime, the "patio party," "cookout," or "backyard picnic," was launched.

In recent years the distinctly American tradition of grilling has been rediscovered and reinterpreted. The shift in the American palate away from canned and frozen foods, preservatives, and foods high in fats and calories has produced the need for a straightforward way of cooking. Grilling is perfect for the fresh fish and produce and high-quality meats and poultry that are becoming more available in our markets. It requires little or no extra fats or oils, and the intense dry heat of the coals sears in natural moisture, heightening the flavor of food.

THE HOWS AND WHYS OF GRILL BOOK

Grill Book draws on the traditions of barbecuing in America, with recipes for grilled steaks, ribs, and chicken. But we also include sections on how to grill all types of meat and poultry, as well as sections on grilling fish, vegetables, and fruit. In Chapter II you will find over thirty recipes for marinades and sauces for grilled foods. Included also are descriptions of the various grills available on the market, and a list of the most essential grill tools. At the end of the section on fuels you will find detailed instructions for lighting the grill and basic grilling techniques. The last chapter contains eighteen full menus, in which at least two or three of the dishes are cooked on the grill.

We grilled all dishes on a kettle grill with a non-movable grill rack fixed 6 inches above the fuel grate. All the food was brought to room temperature before cooking. The grilling days were mostly fine, with little wind and temperatures lingering around 70°. We used mesquite charcoal, which burns slightly hotter than briquets. The cooking times should be longer if you use briquets; gas grills cook hot, so use the times given.

All of our wine recommendations in the chapter "At the Grill" are from California. Similar wines and wines made from the same grape varietals come from all over the world. Don't hesitate to substitute a French Chablis, Italian Soave, German Riesling, or your favorite wine for any of our suggestions.

In addition to new techniques and hints, *Grill Book* is meant to expand your repertoire of foods for the grill and to encourage you to experiment with new tastes. Try grilling oysters in the shell, Japanese eggplant, or sweet pear slices. Or simply marinate and grill your favorite cut of meat, surrounded on the grill by whole scallions or corn in the husk. We've even tried oiled mustard greens on the grill, with amazingly tasty results.

As you gain confidence at the grill and begin to master the techniques of lighting the fire, checking for doneness, controlling flare-ups, and manuevering tricky foods, good grilling will become natural, almost instinctive.

Grilling may seem rustic and primitive (and admittedly a bit messy), but the complex flavors and smells produced by it have an undeniably sensual appeal. The smell of the fire starting and the crackling of the coals are signals to relax and enjoy being outdoors with family, friends, and a glass of wine.

GRILL BOOK

I | Grills, Tools & Fuels

Cooking racks

THE BASIC structure of the grill has changed little over time. It always consists of some form of fuel grate or bed with a cast-iron or steel cooking rack supported over it. Though all grills are based on these components, the shape of a barbecue, the movable parts, the size, width, and what it is made of are all matters of preference (and perhaps a little superstition). Fortunately, for the selective *and* superstitious, dozens of varieties of grills are manufactured. They can be grouped into the general categories of open grills, kettles, hooded grills, portable or table top grills, smokers and Japanese *kamados,* and gas or electric grills.

Always look for good craftsmanship and sturdiness in any grill you are considering. A finish that is heat and rust resistant is essential. Test the movable parts such as vents, hinges, and rack levers to make sure they are easily maneuverable. Look for heat-resistant handles of wood or phenolic plastic. The cooking rack should be porcelain-coated steel, cast iron, or nickel-plated steel, and should be removable but sturdy when in place. The fuel grate should be positioned so that oxygen can freely circulate above and below it.

Open Grills   These grills, sometimes called braziers, do not have hoods. They are most often round, with a single cooking rack supported by a central spindle over a fuel bed rather than a grate. Some open grills have a half-hood or windscreen attached to the side, which helps contain some of the heat. These grills are the least expensive, but are usually

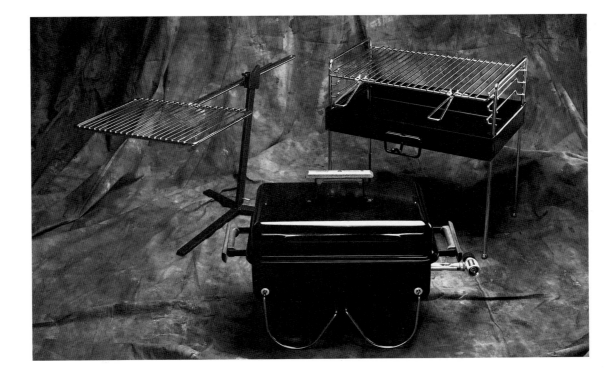

Portable grills

made of thin-gauge metal and are not very sturdy. When selecting an open grill, make sure it is supported by solid legs, so it won't topple or blow over. Since it has no hood, the open grill is best for quick-cooking food that is no more than 1½ inches thick. Drippings from fatty foods such as chicken or sausages will cause flare-ups on an open grill, so be sure to allow the coals to burn to medium-hot before grilling. Have a spray bottle of water on hand as well.

Smoker

Kettles   A kettle acts as a smoker, oven, and grill. The rounded base and hood reflect heat off all inside surfaces, cooking food more quickly and evenly than on an open grill. The smoky flavor is intensified, and the hood eliminates the oxygen that causes flare-ups. Vents in the hood and in the bottom regulate the heat, opening to let oxygen fire up the coals or closing to cool the fire down. The hood can also be left off for open grilling. The disadvantage of the kettle is the hot, unwieldy lid that is rarely hinged onto the base. Most models do, however, have a hook inside the lid for hanging it on the side. Neither the cooking rack nor the fuel grate is adjustable, which limits how close . you can get the food to the fire. Overall, though, the kettle is an exceptional grill for a reasonable price. Kettles come in all sizes, from small totable ones to large backyard size.

Hooded Grills   Square or rectangular grills with hinged hoods also trap heat for faster cooking and smoking, or, left open, cook like an open grill. The mechanisms tend to be more elaborate, however, than on the kettles. The cooking rack and fuel grate are usually adjustable. A few models have fire doors in the side or front for adding charcoal, and some even have temperature gauges on the hood. Many attachments are available for hooded grills, such as rotisseries, warming racks, and side shelves. Hooded grills are available at a wide range of sizes and prices.

Portable Grills   Portable or tabletop grills are distinguished primarily by their size and how easy they are to tote to the beach, picnic, or rooftop. The most familiar grill in this category is the hibachi, but recently other well-made portables have appeared on the market. Portables are typically scaled-down versions of larger open or hooded grills; some have collapsible legs that become handles; others have hinged hoods, adjustable racks, or windscreens. Look for the portable grill that best suits your cooking and transportation needs, and, as always, make sure it is sturdy.

Smokers The smoker is constructed like a tall, cylindrical grill, with the added element of a pan positioned between the fuel grate and the cooking rack for adding liquid. Smokers cook at low temperatures, and the steaming liquid holds in juices while imparting a rich smoky flavor to food. The internal temperature stays around 160° to 200° in a smoker, so gauge your cooking time accordingly. Add more coals and soaked aromatic wood chips (if desired) every 45 minutes or so to keep the smoker going. The smoker can be used as an open grill with the hood off, and the liquid pan can be removed. If the charcoal pan is movable, you can place it in the liquid pan position.

The *kamado* is a Japanese smoker made of very heavy earthenware with a hinged lid. Like a regular smoker, it bakes and smokes simultaneously. *Kamados* can be used as open grills, but the charcoal pan and cooking rack are not adjustable.

You can improvise a smoker with your own covered grill by keeping the coals at the slow-fire stage and the vents half-closed. Allow the coals to reach the slow-fire stage, then arrange them on the fuel grate around a pan half-filled with liquid. Place the roast or large bird over the pan. Keep the internal temperature just under 200°, and add hot coals every 45 minutes to 1 hour.

Gas and Electric Grills The designs for gas and electric grills are based on the hooded and kettle grills, with some type of permanent briquet-shaped rocks heated by gas or an electric coil to substitute for charcoal. They heat up quickly and are less fuss, but also require a natural-gas hook-up or cannister, or an electrical outlet. The smoke created by juices or fat dripping on the hot "coals" does impart some smoky flavor, but the full flavors of hardwood charcoals and aromatic chips are missing. Gas grills cook at temperatures between 700° and 900°, which is slightly hotter than a briquet fire, and almost as hot as a hardwood charcoal fire (see Fuels, page 23). Gas and electric grills make barbecuing easier, but compromise on flavor.

Kettle grills

Tools for the grill

L ONG-HANDLED TOOLS are ideal for grilling, as they are designed to keep your hands away from the hot coals. Sturdiness is another essential quality in a grill tool. You won't want it bending or falling apart when you are handling hot grills or food. Look for good-quality grill tools in hardware stores, and sometimes cookware or restaurant supply stores. Many grill manufacturers also sell a line of grill tools (these are mentioned in Sources, along with mail-order information).

Mitt A fireproof mitt should be your first grill tool. With a good mitt you can handle hot hoods, cooking racks, spits, skewers, chimneys, drip pans, and even coals if your mitt is well insulated. No grill should be without a mitt or two nearby.

Tongs We like the long-handled, spring-loaded tongs that you can use, with your mitt, to do a wide variety of tasks *safely*. Use them to move coals, turn food on the grill, and, with the hollow "spoon side" of the tong, baste food as it grills.

Spray Bottle A spray bottle filled with water comes in handy for flare-ups and errant sparks. For flare-ups, set the spray jet on its narrowest stream, and aim right for the spot where the fat is dripping on the hot coal (avoid dousing the entire fire).

Wire Brush This tool makes a messy but essential task easier. The cooking rack should be scraped clean before you grill *each time*. Not only does burnt-on grease impart an unpleasant flavor to food, but food tends to stick to a dirty rack. Use the steel plate attached to the top of the wire brush to scrape off tough char, then go over the front and back of the rack with the brush. Rub off excess grease with crumpled newspapers or paper towels. Treat the rack like a cast-iron pan by oiling it from time to time to season it. To clean the brush, run it under *very* hot water for a minute or so to rinse out the grease. In lieu of a wire brush try crumpled aluminum foil to scrape the rack.

Marinade Pans We encourage you to invest in one or two large rectangular pans of porcelain or enamel, or glass baking dishes. Avoid untreated aluminum, which reacts with acidic marinades and can darken food and impart a slightly metallic flavor. Disposable aluminum pans with a shiny finish are suitable for all types of marinades since the aluminum has been treated. Use glass, porcelain, or stainless steel bowls for food in pieces or chunks, or food that doesn't need to lie flat. When marinating foods in the refrigerator, cover the pan with aluminum foil and poke a few holes in the top to allow air to circulate around the food.

Skewers Wood or bamboo skewers are excellent for lightweight, quick-cooking foods such as vegetable chunks, thin strips of chicken or beef, and seafood. Soak wood skewers in water for 15 minutes or so to keep them from burning on the grill. Wood skewers are also useful for testing doneness. A poke with a skewer will tell you if vegetables are done; you can test chicken by piercing the meat near a bone to see if the juices run clear; and fish is easily checked by gently prying apart the layers with a skewer. Metal skewers have a wider blade and are sturdier than wood ones. Use them for weighty food such as beef chunks, or for long skewered dishes. Metal skewers with decorated handles make an attractive presentation.

Basting brush Use basting brushes to brush on thin layers of marinade, sauce, butter, or oil. They come in a variety of sizes, but we like either long-handled brushes with a 45-degree bend near the bristles, or long-handled round brushes. We also like those brushes on which the ring, or tang, that holds the bristles to the handle is sealed—this keeps food particles from getting trapped under it.

Flashlight   This may seem like an odd piece of equipment on a list of grill tools, but suffice it to say that a flashlight can come in very handy when the sun goes down.

Brushes and tongs

Spatulas   Tender pieces of food, especially fish, require careful turning with a spatula so they won't fall apart on the grill. An excellent grill spatula is one with an extra-long blade and a crooked handle for maneuvering around the grill. You can successfully pick up a whole fish or large fillet on a long-bladed spatula.

Long-handled Forks and Spoons   Though they come in almost every "barbecue set," we find long-handled forks and spoons to have limited use. However, when tongs are out of reach, you can use forks to turn vegetables and heavy foods, but avoid poking meat as it cooks. Use spoons for basting on the grill.

Knives   A good set of sharp knives is always an essential cooking tool. You will be able to slice vegetables evenly and safely, cut up meats and poultry, and, with a sharp, thin-bladed knife, make a small, nearly invisible cut into your steak to see if it's perfectly done.

Drip Pans   Disposable aluminum pans make the best drip pans for the grill. They are available in almost any grocery store for a reasonable price. These pans, which are made of treated aluminum, can also be used as marinade pans. The use of drip pans is explained on page 29.

Hinged Grills   Hinged grills, whether square, round, rectangular, or fish-shaped, all function the same way: two thin wire racks hinged at the side hold food between them. Some kind of catch, either on the side or on the handle, secures the two racks together. Place it right on the grill, and turn the food by turning the hinged grill itself. Oil the racks beforehand so food will not stick.

Thermometer   Invest in a good-quality, quick-reading meat and poultry thermometer if you plan to cook a lot of roasts and large birds. It must be used on meat more than 2 inches thick to be effective.

Carving Board   We like the boards with a juice catcher (carved into the wood like a canal) for saving precious juices to spoon over meat after it is carved.

H IGH-QUALITY efficient fuel is the most important ingredient for good grilling. Charcoal is the most common, but it varies widely in content, quality, price, and availability, and choosing the best type is not always easy. Lump charcoal is created by slowly smoldering wood in a low-oxygen fire. The carbon that remains re-lights faster and burns hotter and cleaner than wood. Left in this pure state, charcoal is a clean and efficient fuel, but unfortunately the modern charcoal briquet has been stretched with fillers and binders.

Briquets   Charcoal briquets were invented back in 1923 by Henry Ford, but *not* for grilling! He discovered that by pulverizing lump charcoal (which was a by-product of the production of wood alcohol, the fuel he used in auto manufacture) and binding it together in even little bricks, he had created an efficient industrial fuel.

Ford's charcoal business faltered, and in the 1950s the Kingsford Company took his invention and marketed it as the "barbecue briquet" to meet the emerging outdoor grilling trend. The immediate success of the briquet established it as the dominant grilling fuel.

The charcoal briquet is now made from wood scraps that are smoldered into carbon. These are often mixed with some type of filler, then bound with starch, and pressed into briquet shape. Many briquets contain a chemical additive to promote faster lighting.

Steer away from briquets with a high filler or chemical additive content, or those that contain raw coal. These give food a distinctly unpleasant taste and sometimes a greasy residue. If you must use briquets, *always* wait until the coals have a coating of gray ash. While black is still showing, the binders and fillers are still burning, and the unpleasant taste from them may be imparted to food.

Hardwood Charcoal   Hardwood charcoal is made directly from whole pieces of wood—no additives or filler, just pure charcoal. Common sources of this charcoal are mesquite, oak, maple, cherry, and hickory wood. Don't be surprised if you find some tree limbs that are intact, although carbonized and black. Break up pieces larger than a grapefruit for faster lighting and a more even fire.

Hardwood charcoal burns hotter and cleaner than briquets, and leaves no unpleasant taste or residue. One grill manufacturer, who has used only hardwood charcoal since the 1940s, says that hardwood charcoal has an average "ash content" of only 6 percent, compared with a 25 percent ash content in briquets. This means that roughly 15 to 25 percent of the briquet is dropping down into the ash-catcher rather than burning in the fuel grate and producing heat to grill with. In addition to this loss in effectiveness, briquets burn at temperatures 200° to 300° *lower* than hardwood charcoal, thus requiring more briquets over a longer period of time. Hardwood charcoal is reusable, sometimes even a second and third time. Briquets are very seldom effective the second time.

Mesquite Mesquite charcoal is rapidly becoming the most popular hardwood charcoal on the market, primarily because the wood itself is more abundant and therefore cheaper than other hardwoods in many parts of the country.

Mesquite grows in this country in arid regions of the Southwest, but most of it comes from Mexico. Among the largest producers of mesquite charcoal are the Yaqui Indians of north central Mexico. Following the same production method they have used for generations, they carefully pile hand-felled mesquite into large mounds and smolder it for weeks under an airtight covering of clay and straw.

Mesquite charcoal burns very cleanly and with little smoke at temperatures ranging from 800° to 1000°. A common misconception about mesquite charcoal is that it gives off a strong and unpleasant odor and flavor. Mesquite *charcoal* is in fact very subtle, and lightly flavors food. Burning mesquite *wood* produces much more smoke, which gives food a stronger flavor. It is by no means unpleasant, but if you use mesquite wood chips, select foods that will stand up to its distinctive, woody flavor.

When lighting mesquite charcoal, be prepared for some dramatic snapping and crackling. This is one of its characteristics, so stand back a bit and make sure that flammable items are clear of the grill. (See Sources for suppliers of hardwood charcoal and mesquite.)

Wood Woods such as oak, cherry, alder, hickory, and maple can also be used to cook with, although they don't burn as hot as charcoal. Light wood chunks and allow them to burn until red hot and lightly covered with gray ash (about 45 minutes). You are ready to cook when it reaches this stage, but remember that it will burn up more quickly than charcoal, so gauge your cooking time accordingly.

Smoking or Flavor Chips The most common smoking chips are woods such as hickory, mesquite, oak, cherry, maple, aspen, or apple. When used in moderation, smoking chips can give food just the right distinctive taste. For the most smoke, soak the chips in water for ½ hour before tossing on the fire (though too many wet chips on a hot fire may extinguish the coals). For a quick flash of smoke, toss on a few dry chips. They burn up rapidly and give off just a little flavor. Dried grapevine gives off a subtle, almost sweet smoke and can be used without soaking.

Both fresh and dried aromatic herbs such as bay leaves, or sprigs of thyme, rosemary, or sage, can be tossed on the coals to lightly flavor food.

Charcoal, kindling, and smoking chips

Fire-starting equipment

*Newspaper "pretzels"
for lighting coals*

LIGHTING THE GRILL

How Many Coals?

Visualize the area on the cooking rack that the food will occupy. Make a two-deep bed of coals extending about an inch or so beyond that area. Keep in mind that if the cooking time goes beyond 45 minutes to 1 hour, you will need to add more charcoal, allowing 15 minutes for new coals to ignite.

Fire-Starting Equipment

We strongly favor using kindling, a chimney, or an electric coil, as they are safe, fast, and do not add a chemical odor or taste to food. As a general rule, leave any cover off and any bottom vents open when lighting the fire.

Kindling   This method requires a bit of practice to master, but it is the fastest. Beginning at the top corner of a large sheet of newspaper, roll the paper diagonally into a tube. Fold the ends over each other, making a pretzel shape. Place 2 or 3 of these newspaper "pretzels" in the bottom of the fuel grate or grill bed. Place uniform pieces of wood kindling, such as dry twigs and sticks or scrap lumber pieces, over the paper. Over this, carefully position 5 or 6 coals in a pyramid so that there is some space for air between them. Ignite the newspaper. As the fire builds, add more coals to the pile. When the coals are hot, spread them out for a nice, even coal bed.

Chimney   The chimney is a cylinder of heavy metal on short legs, with holes punched on the sides for ventilation. We like those with a grate on the inside about three-quarters down to hold the coals. Stuff a loosely crumpled sheet of newspaper in the bottom of the chimney and place it on the fuel grate or the grill bed if there is no grate. Pile coals into the top of the chimney. Open any vents in the bottom of the grill, and ignite the paper. Air is directed up the chimney, and in a very short time the coals will begin to light. Most chimneys have handles to pour the coals out into the fuel grate or grill bed; if yours does not, lift the chimney with sturdy tongs or an insulated mitt. Be sure to put this hot piece of equipment out of the way.

Electric Starter   This is a clean, fast, and relatively safe method of lighting coals. The starter is an oval-shaped heating element attached to a long handle with a cord. Nestle the unit in among the coals on the fuel grate, and plug it into an electrical outlet. It heats to red hot, igniting the coals directly touching it. Other coals are ignited by the lit coals, so this method takes a bit longer than kindling or the chimney. Its primary drawback is that it requires a nearby outlet. The manufacturer recommends keeping the unit on no longer than 10 minutes.

Fluid and Block Starters   Fluid starter is the most common method of lighting charcoal fires. Unfortunately, it adds a chemical solution to the coals which you must allow to *completely* burn off if you want to avoid giving food a chemical taste. If you use it, use it safely. Place 6 or 7 coals in the bottom of the fuel grate or on the grill bed and douse them with starter. Pile the rest of the coals on top, forming a pyramid. Ignite the bottom coals that have been treated. They will flame up, lighting the others. *Do not* squirt starter on a flaming fire.

Block starters are usually chemically treated with a substance that lights easily. To use, place one or two among the coals and ignite. Allow it to burn down completely before cooking.

When Is the Fire Ready?

Most charcoal, whether briquets or hardwood, requires 30 to 45 minutes to thoroughly light. While the coals are igniting you will notice flames licking up around the sides. While the fire is still flaming, it is not quite ready.

Coals are at the *red-hot* stage when they are red and glowing with an occasional flame-up, and have a light layer of gray ash. You will not be able to hold your hand 6 inches above the coals for more than about 3 seconds. You can cook fish and very quick-cooking non-fatty foods, such as thin strips of meat or poultry, over this fire.

Almost all grilling is done when the coals are *medium-hot*. They will have a layer of gray ash through which a red glow is occasionally visible. You will not be able to hold your hand over this fire for longer than 5 to 6 seconds. Use a *slow fire* for long-cooking foods such as roasts and large birds. The coals will have a thick layer of gray ash, with almost no red visible.

To cool the fire down, cover the grill if possible and close any vents down by half, and allow it to burn a little longer before cooking. You can also spread the coals out for a less intense bed of heat (use this technique if your grill doesn't have a hood). If your fire is too slow, open the vents and hood and allow the circulating air to flame it up again. Tapping the coals with a long-handled tool will knock some of the ash off and heat the fire up a bit as well. If the fire has burned down too far, add more coals and allow 15 to 20 minutes with the vents and hood open for them to start. If possible, try to add coals before you begin cooking. Otherwise, keep the food to one side of the grill for the first 10 minutes as new coals ignite.

To "Turn Off" the Grill

Immediately after cooking, cover the grill and close down all the vents. Omitting oxygen will extinguish the coals. Since hardwood charcoal is reusable, this simple habit will give you two to three times more use. If you have cooked on an open grill, douse the coals lightly with water. Coals will be reusable when thoroughly dried out. When relighting used hardwood coals, combine them with fresh ones, as used charcoal takes longer to light and doesn't burn as hot as unused coals.

QUESTIONS, ANSWERS, AND ADVICE

Open or Covered?

There are two approaches to cooking on most grills: *open,* with the hood up or off; and *covered,* with the hood down. If your grill has no hood, your only option is open grilling.

The coals are hotter and more prone to flare-ups on an open grill because of the increased draft around them. Food cooks quickly on the outside and becomes slightly charred. This light char seals in juices, leaving the inside succulent and tender. Open grilling is best for

food no more than 1½ inches thick, such as fish fillets, shellfish, vegetable slices, steaks, chops, and skewered dishes. These foods cook through in under 8 to 10 minutes per side and benefit from the quick seal on the outside.

Some foods cook more evenly on a closed grill. These include thick fish steaks, roasts, chicken, duck, and whole vegetables. On an open grill, food thicker than 1½ inches will be done on the outside long before the inside is cooked. Inside a covered grill the heat circulates all around the food, cooking it more quickly and evenly.

Foods such as chicken (with the skin on) produce too much fat for open grilling. Fat is highly flammable and causes flare-ups that char the outside while the inside remains raw. The hood acts as a snuffer, preventing the oxygen from flaming the coals.

Follow these guidelines when deciding between open and covered grilling:

• If the food is no thicker than 1½ inches and will cook sufficiently through on the inside before charring on the outside, it qualifies for open grilling.

• If the food tends to dry out on the grill, cook it covered.

• If the food is fatty and will cause excessive flare-ups, or if you plan to baste frequently with an oily marinade or sauce, cook on a covered grill.

If you are in the process of grilling and are having too many flare-ups, cover the grill and close down the vents by half to cool the fire down. When in doubt, *remove the food!* Then cover the grill and close down the vents completely. The food can go back on the grill to finish cooking when the coals are not so hot, usually after 5 to 10 minutes.

Direct or Indirect Cooking?

The two methods of cooking over the coals are grilling *directly* over them, and *indirectly* over them.

Most grilling is done by direct heat. Food is placed on the cooking rack directly above the hot coals, which provides the most intense heat. The grill can be open or covered depending on the thickness and fat content of the food (see above). We recommend direct heat for foods that require a cooking time of less than 30 minutes, such as steaks, fish, chicken, chops, and vegetables.

You can create two cooking temperatures on the grill by piling more coals on one side of the fuel grate than on the other. Thus, the hotter side of the grill can be used for searing and quick-cooking foods. Move foods cooking too quickly to the medium-hot side, or use it for grilling longer-cooking foods.

Use *indirect* heat for roasts and large whole birds, and foods that require longer cooking time and even, less intense heat. Arrange the hot coals to the sides of the fuel grate. Place the food on the cooking rack over the center, or where the heat is least direct.

The cover is always used for indirect cooking to provide an even temperature inside the grill. Replenish the coals every 45 minutes to 1 hour to keep the fire going. If possible, add *hot* coals that you have started in a chimney.

A drip pan may be placed on the fuel grate between the coals to collect drippings for fatty foods such as chicken, duck, or leg of lamb. This keeps the grill clean and minimizes flare-ups. To cook with moist heat, add liquid such as water, wine, or broth to the drip pan. Replenish the liquid as it evaporates, every half hour or so. Add aromatic herbs to the liquid for more flavorful steam.

Searing

Searing is a preliminary grilling step used to quickly seal the outside of food. To sear, grill food over a red-hot fire with the cover off for approximately 1 to 2 minutes per side. The seal prevents juices from running out and moisture from evaporating as the food cooks. Sear foods that tend to dry out, such as pork chops, most poultry, and large roasts. You can also sear steaks, chops, and vegetables to help seal in juices. Always have food at room temperature and oil the cooking rack before searing to keep it from sticking. Do not sear fish or foods that may break up if turned too often.

Oiling the Cooking Rack

It never hurts to lightly brush the hot cooking rack with oil just before cooking to discourage food from sticking. We have an inexpensive long-handled brush set aside specifically for this task. Use a mitt, and avoid overloading the brush with oil, as the drips will cause flare-ups. Always oil the rack before cooking fish and chicken. Oiling the rack will help to season it as well.

Grill Advice

Allow an hour between starting the coals and actually cooking, both to prepare the food for the grill and to allow the coals to burn to the right stage for grilling. Coals require between 30 and 45 minutes to get hot, and you can add to that the 15 or so minutes it takes to prepare the grill itself (scraping the rack, emptying the ashes, setting up the fire, and so on).

• Position the grill away from your house, dry leaves, or anything that a spark might ignite. Do not interpret the term "tailgate party" too literally: move the grill well away from the back of the car. Remember also to keep children and pets away from hot grills and equipment.

• Watch the grill at all times. If not you, then someone should have an eye on the hot grill all the time it is in use. This is not only for safety, but also to guard against ruinous flare-ups.

• Have your grill tools nearby. One way to guarantee that you will leave the grill is to leave your tools in the house, so have everything you need out next to the grill before you start.

• Keep the grill clean. The black buildup on the cooking rack is *not* what adds that distinctive flavor characteristic of grilling, and it also encourages food to stick. The rack should be cleaned with a wire brush before or after grilling. Season the rack by regularly oiling it and by keeping it free of charred buildup and grease. Empty the ash-catcher before grilling so that oxygen can freely flow around the coals to keep them going.

2 | Marinades & Sauces

Tools for the kitchen

A MARINADE generally describes a paste or liquid mixture that food soaks in before grilling. The soaking time can be anywhere from 15 minutes to 48 hours. The oil in marinades lubricates food and gives it flavor. The acidic elements of a marinade are commonly wine, vinegar, soy sauce, mustard, citrus juice, or yogurt. They permeate tissue and break down tough fibers, thus tenderizing meat and leaving it lightly flavored. The ratio of oil to acid depends in part on the food to be marinated. For example, a tough cut of beef requires more wine than oil, and would benefit most by marinating overnight. Fish, on the other hand, should stand no longer than 30 minutes and only in oil-based marinades. Acidic substances can actually "cook" the fish, as in *ceviche*.

If you are planning to marinate for only a short time, mix the marinade an hour in advance to allow the flavors to infuse and mellow. Never add salt to a marinade, as it draws out the moisture essential to keeping meat juicy and tender. Salt food only after it is grilled. You may even find that the smoky flavor imparted by the coals is an excellent salt substitute.

Marinate meat and poultry at room temperature for up to 3 hours, or in the refrigerator for up to 48 hours for maximum flavor. Marinate fish and shellfish no longer than 30 minutes at room temperature (or 2 hours in the refrigerator). *Always* remove food from the refrigerator 30 minutes before grilling to bring it to room temperature. A refrigerator-cold piece of fish or meat may overcook on the outside before it is done on the inside.

Bowls and rectangular baking dishes made of glass, enamel, porcelain, or treated aluminum (see Marinade Pans, page 21) are ideal for marinades. Select pans in which the meat and fish fit snugly but lie flat. The marinade should come up around the edges of the food but need not cover it. Turn food several times as it marinates. Larger roasts can be marinated in a large leakproof plastic bag. Put the marinade and meat together in the bag, squeeze out most of the air, and seal tightly with a rubber band. Turn the bag from time to time to distribute the marinade evenly.

Any marinade can be used to baste on foods during grilling to add moisture and flavor. Use a brush to baste, or spoon on very small amounts, as the oils in marinades will cause flare-ups. You need only baste every 5 to 7 minutes, or once before the food is turned and once after.

WHITE WINE MARINADE   1½ cups

White wine marinade is an excellent basic marinade for all types of poultry and the more oily types of fish such as shellfish, salmon, and trout, and to baste on vegetables. Ours is flavored with tarragon, but try also fresh or dried basil, rosemary, or thyme. Use onions or garlic rather than shallots, and try different wine varietals for new effects. For a fish marinade, decrease the wine and vinegar to 2 tablespoons of each.

> ½ cup dry white wine
> ½ cup white wine vinegar or champagne vinegar
> ½ cup olive oil
> 2 shallots, coarsely chopped
> 3 teaspoons chopped fresh tarragon, or 1 teaspoon dried

Combine all the ingredients in a bowl. Whisk to emulsify.

RED WINE MARINADE — 2½ cups

Any cut of meat that needs tenderizing takes well to this marinade. Varying the ingredients will add delicate shades of flavor to meat. For example, a heavy Cabernet wine will produce a much different marinade than a Pinot Noir or Zinfandel. Try adding fresh chopped mint to a lamb marinade, or sliced apples to one for pork. For large roasts, double the recipe, using a whole bottle of wine.

1½ cups dry red wine
¼ cup red wine vinegar
½ cup olive oil
1 small onion, sliced
1 carrot, sliced into coins
1 bay leaf, torn in half
1 teaspoon black peppercorns, crushed

Combine all the ingredients in a bowl. Whisk to emulsify.

SESAME MARINADE — 2½ cups

Flank steak stands up best to the full, smoky flavor of sesame oil. This recipe calls for dark sesame oil, made from roasted sesame seeds. You can find it in Asian or specialty markets. Sesame Marinade makes enough for 2 medium-sized flank steaks.

1 cup dry red wine
¾ cup red wine vinegar
¼ cup dark sesame oil
½ cup olive oil
6 garlic cloves, sliced into ovals
3 tablespoons coarsely chopped fresh ginger
3 teaspoons fresh thyme, or 1 teaspoon dried

Combine all the ingredients in a bowl. Whisk to emulsify. Marinate flank steak overnight in a flat pan before grilling.

HERBED OIL MARINADE — ½ cup

Grapeseed oil is light, with a slightly nutty flavor perfect for fish. Use this oil marinade for leaner types of fish such as sea bass, swordfish, rockfish, angler or monkfish, and tilefish.

½ cup grapeseed oil
Dash of white wine vinegar
1 teaspoon chopped fresh or crumbled dried herb
A few drops of lemon juice

Combine all the ingredients in a bowl. Whisk to emulsify. Marinate fish for 15 to 30 minutes before grilling, or use the herbed oil to baste food just before and during grilling.

PEANUT MARINADE — 2 cups

The traditional thick dipping sauce for *satay,* the Indonesian skewered beef dish, is the inspiration for this marinade. To create *satay* skewers, thread thin, 1-inch-wide slices of marinated beef or chicken onto wood skewers and grill them 2 minutes per side over red-hot coals. Serve the marinade as a dipping sauce, if desired.

½ cup chunky peanut butter (no salt or sugar added)
½ cup peanut oil
¼ cup white wine vinegar
¼ cup tamari (see note)
¼ cup fresh lemon juice
4 garlic cloves, minced
8 cilantro sprigs, minced
1 whole dried red chili pepper, minced, or 2 teaspoons dried red pepper flakes
2 teaspoons chopped fresh ginger

Combine all the ingredients in a blender or food processor. Blend well to emulsify, adding a few drops of water if the mixture is too thick. Marinate beef or chicken overnight.

Note: Tamari is a strong soy sauce found in Asian and specialty markets. Use soy sauce if *tamari* is unavailable.

ZINFANDEL SAUCE — 4 cups

A variation on the basic red wine marinade, this sauce is both an excellent marinade and a delicious sauce to serve over grilled lamb or beef. This recipe makes a large quantity—enough for 1 leg of lamb, a beef loin roast, or 2 flank steaks.

1 bottle Zinfandel
¼ cup red wine vinegar
¼ cup rice vinegar or distilled white vinegar
¼ cup olive oil
2 tablespoons dark sesame oil
6 garlic cloves, sliced into ovals
3 teaspoons chopped fresh rosemary, or 1 teaspoon dried
Freshly ground pepper

Combine all the ingredients in a bowl. Whisk to emulsify. Marinate lamb or beef for 2 hours to overnight before grilling. *To make the sauce:* Reserve ¼ cup of the marinade to use as a baste on grilling meat. Pour the remaining marinade into a non-aluminum saucepan. Simmer gently and reduce by half, or until the sauce has thickened. Serve over sliced grilled lamb or beef.

RASPBERRY VINEGAR MARINADE — 1¾ cups

The fruity flavor of this marinade complements poultry, especially Cornish game hens and small game birds. For a more pronounced raspberry flavor, add ½ cup lightly mashed fresh raspberries to the marinade.

¾ cup red raspberry vinegar
½ cup dry white wine
¼ cup olive oil
Juice of ¼ lemon
2 shallots, coarsely chopped
2 tablespoons chopped fresh basil, or 2 teaspoons dried
Freshly ground pepper

Combine all the ingredients in a bowl. Whisk to emulsify. Marinate poultry up to 4 hours.

SHERRY VINEGAR, PORT, AND PRUNE MARINADE
1¼ cups

Prunes flavor the hearty wine, creating a full-bodied wine marinade for any cut of pork.

½ cup sherry vinegar
1 cup port wine
¼ cup olive oil
2 tablespoons honey
3 teaspoons chopped fresh thyme,
*   or 1 teaspoon dried*
1 dozen whole dried pitted prunes

Combine all the ingredients in a bowl. Whisk to emulsify. Marinate pork 1 to 3 hours before grilling. Spoon the marinade over grilled pork and garnish with the prunes.

HONEY, TAMARI, AND ORANGE MARINADE
2 cups

Keep in mind that sugar burns easily on the grill, so use this marinade on quick-cooking foods such as boned chicken, split Cornish game hens, squab, flank steak, or pre-baked ribs.

1 cup fresh orange juice
2 tablespoons peanut oil
¼ cup white wine vinegar
3 tablespoons tamari or soy sauce
1 tablespoon raw honey
Freshly ground white pepper

Combine all the ingredients in a bowl. Whisk to emulsify. Marinate poultry from 1 to 4 hours before grilling. Marinate flank steak and ribs overnight.

NAM PRIK MARINADE
1 cup

Nam prik is a Thai term for "spicy," usually describing a hot paste made of ground red chilies and oil. Red chili paste can be found in Asian specialty markets. This is an excellent marinade for all types of shellfish, and is especially delicious with shrimp.

½ cup rice vinegar or distilled white vinegar
Juice of ½ lemon
¼ cup olive oil
1 green and 1 red hot serrano chili (or any hot
*   or mild chili pepper), seeded and slivered*
½ teaspoon dried red pepper flakes
3 slices lemon zest
1 tablespoon nam prik red chili paste

Combine all the ingredients in a bowl. Mix well. Let stand 30 minutes before using. Marinate shellfish 30 minutes before grilling.

Marinade ingredients

MUSTARD MARINADE   2 cups

This thick marinade of many mustards is delicious on chicken, and it can also be served as a sauce over plain grilled food.

¼ cup Dijon mustard
¼ cup whole-seed mustard (also called "old-style")
¼ cup hot German mustard
¼ cup distilled white vinegar
¼ cup olive oil
½ cup apple juice (preferably unsweetened)
Juice of ½ lemon
1 whole shallot, sliced into rings
Freshly ground pepper

Combine all the ingredients in a bowl. Whisk to emulsify. Marinate chicken 1 to 3 hours before grilling.

WALNUT MARINADE   1 cup

Walnut oil is a luxurious oil, nutty and full-flavored but amazingly light and smooth. It burns easily, so use this marinade on quick-cooking foods such as fish fillets, vegetables, and boned chicken breasts.

¼ cup walnut oil
¼ cup corn, safflower, or peanut oil
¼ cup white wine vinegar
2 tablespoons chopped fresh basil,
   or 2 teaspoons dried
½ cup coarsely chopped walnuts
Freshly ground pepper

Combine all the ingredients in a bowl. Whisk to emulsify. Marinate fish or chicken 15 to 30 minutes before grilling, or baste while grilling.

ESCAVECHE MARINADE   3 cups

This tart marinade is great with fish and chicken. Prepare the marinade the day before if possible to allow all the flavors to mingle. Serve the onion and pepper slices over the grilled fish or chicken as a garnish.

1 cup olive oil
2½ cups dry white wine
4 limes, cut into ¼-inch slices
2 yellow onions, cut into ¼-inch slices
2 green bell peppers, seeded and sliced into rings
8 garlic cloves, sliced into rings
20 whole cloves
8 cilantro sprigs, coarsely chopped

Combine the oil and wine in a bowl and whisk to emulsify. Add the limes, onions, peppers, garlic, cloves, and cilantro and refrigerate, covered, overnight. Marinate chicken 30 minutes to 1 hour before grilling; marinate fish no longer than 10 minutes. Use the marinade as a basting sauce while grilling.

LEMON MARINADE   1½ cups

This tangy lemon marinade is very good with chicken or veal.

½ cup olive oil
Juice of 2 lemons
¼ cup dry white wine
1 garlic clove, minced
3 teaspoons fresh sage, or 1 teaspoon dried
Zest of 1 whole lemon
1 bay leaf, torn in half
Freshly ground white pepper

Combine all the ingredients in a bowl. Whisk to emulsify. Marinate chicken or veal 30 minutes before grilling.

LIME MARINADE   1 cup

Limes add a delightful flavor to grilled chicken, giving it a fresh, tangy flavor reminiscent of chicken dishes from Mexico.

½ cup peanut oil
Juice of 2 limes
1 tablespoon white wine vinegar
1 teaspoon honey
¼ cup coarsely chopped onion
Freshly ground white pepper

Combine all the ingredients in a bowl. Whisk to emulsify. Marinate chicken for 30 minutes to 1 hour before grilling.

ASIAN BARBECUE MARINADE   2½ cups

Asian Barbecue Marinade combines sweet and spicy flavors for chicken, pork, flank steak, or strips of beef. The *hoisin* sauce, a sweet bean paste, is a common flavor in Asian cuisines and can be found in ethnic markets and the specialty section of some grocery stores, as can the hot chili oil.

½ cup peanut oil
¼ cup hoisin sauce
¼ cup soy sauce
½ cup rice vinegar or distilled white vinegar
¼ cup rice wine or dry sherry
½ teaspoon hot chili oil, optional
Dash of dark sesame oil, optional
2 whole scallions, minced
2 garlic cloves, minced
2 tablespoons minced fresh ginger

Combine all the ingredients in a bowl and mix well. Marinate chicken, pork, flank steak, or beef overnight in the refrigerator. Use the marinade to baste the food as it grills.

TARRAGON MARINADE   2½ cups

The rich sweet flavor of tarragon goes well with rabbit, chicken, veal, or pork. Try marinating food overnight for the full flavor of the tarragon.

½ cup olive oil
1 cup dry white wine
½ cup champagne vinegar or white wine vinegar
2 shallots, minced
2 tablespoons chopped fresh tarragon,
   or 2 teaspoons dried

Combine all the ingredients in a bowl. Whisk to emulsify. Marinate food 1 hour to overnight before grilling.

MARSALA MARINADE

2 cups

Marsala is a fortified red wine from southern Italy, most famous for its role in the delicious custard dessert, *zabaione*. Like sherry, Marsala is slightly sweet with a medium body and makes a particularly flavorful marinade for all types of poultry. Serve grilled Marsala chicken pieces over pasta, boiled and tossed with *crème fraîche* (see page 39), freshly grated Parmesan cheese, fresh chopped parsley, and plenty of cracked pepper.

1½ cups Marsala
½ cup olive oil
3 garlic cloves, chopped
1 teaspoon fennel seed
3 teaspoons chopped fresh oregano,
*   or 1 teaspoon dried*
2 dashes Worcestershire sauce
Freshly ground pepper

Combine all the ingredients in a bowl. Whisk to emulsify. Marinate poultry 4 hours before grilling.

SAUCES

S AUCES may be basted on during grilling, spooned over grilled food, or both. Use sauces that are oil- or butter-based for basting. Foods basted with sauces containing more than a dash of honey or sugar should be either grilled over a medium-hot to slow fire or on a covered grill, or the sauce should be brushed on only toward the end of grilling, as sugar burns easily and can give food a slightly burnt taste on the outside. Compound butters add delicate flavor to grilled food, while cold sauces such as aïoli, *pesto,* and salsa are assertive accompaniments, perfect for foods that have not been marinated.

WHITE WINE BUTTER SAUCE
LEMON BUTTER SAUCE 1 cup

This rich buttery sauce is perfect for seafood, especially shellfish. Brush it on (liberally) as food grills, and for a real splurge, use it after grilling as a dipping sauce.

1 stick (½ cup) butter
4 garlic cloves, minced
¼ cup dry white wine
Juice of ½ lemon
Dash of salt
Freshly ground white pepper

In a heavy non-aluminum saucepan, cook the garlic in butter over very low heat for 2 to 3 minutes (do not allow the butter to brown). Whisk in the wine and lemon juice and remove from the heat. Season to taste. This can be done right on the grill if you have the space. Note: For Lemon Butter Sauce use 1 clove garlic, eliminate wine and use juice of 1 lemon.

RED WINE BUTTER SAUCE 1 cup

This red wine counterpart to our White Wine Butter Sauce is for beef, pork, and lamb. Baste it on during grilling.

6 tablespoons butter
1 tablespoon olive oil
4 shallots, coarsely chopped
1½ cups dry red wine
Salt and freshly ground white pepper

Melt 1 tablespoon of the butter with the oil in a large heavy non-aluminum saucepan. Sauté the shallots until translucent, approximately 15 minutes. Whisk in the red wine and simmer until reduced by half. Strain the liquid, return it to the saucepan, and over low heat whisk in the remaining butter tablespoon by tablespoon. Season to taste.

RED PEPPER BUTTER SAUCE
1½ cups

The sweet flavor of roasted red pepper comes through in this butter sauce, which is especially delicious over grilled fish. This sauce can be basted on during grilling, spooned over plain grilled fish, or both.

½ cup roasted, peeled, and seeded red bell peppers
6 tablespoons butter
2 tablespoons olive oil
3 shallots, chopped
1 teaspoon honey
Dash of salt
Freshly ground pepper

Coarsely chop the red peppers and set aside. In a medium saucepan, melt the butter over low heat, add the oil, and sauté the shallots until softened but not brown. Remove from the heat, stir in the honey until dissolved, and cool slightly. In a blender or food processor, purée the peppers, and while the machine is running on low, slowly pour in the butter mixture and blend until emulsified. Scrape into a bowl and season to taste. For a creamier sauce (but one not to be used as a baste), heat the sauce slightly and whisk in ½ cup heavy cream.

TRADITIONAL BARBECUE SAUCE
4 cups

Delicious on ribs and chicken, our Traditional Barbecue Sauce is slightly sweet and not too spicy (to heat things up a bit, try the next sauce).

2 tablespoons butter
2 tablespoons olive oil
1 medium-sized onion, minced
2 garlic cloves, minced
¾ cup red wine vinegar
1 cup beer
½ cup dry red wine
2 large ripe tomatoes, minced
1 can tomato paste
3 tablespoons brown sugar
2 tablespoons Worcestershire sauce
1 tablespoon whole-grain mustard
6 to 8 dashes Tabasco sauce
1 teaspoon ground cloves
Dash of salt
Freshly ground pepper

Melt the butter and oil in a large heavy non-aluminum saucepan. Sauté the onion until translucent, approximately 10 minutes. Add the garlic and sauté a few minutes more. Add the remaining ingredients, stirring well to

combine. Simmer for 30 minutes, stirring occasionally. Marinate ribs or chicken from 1 hour to overnight, as desired.

NEW AMERICAN
SPICY BARBECUE SAUCE 4 cups

A bit hotter than the Traditional Barbecue Sauce. To add even more heat, sprinkle in extra Tabasco, cayenne, or dried red pepper flakes.

2 tablespoons butter
2 tablespoons olive oil
1 medium-sized onion, minced
2 garlic cloves, minced
¼ cup red wine vinegar
½ cup dry red wine
1 cup water
2 large ripe tomatoes, minced
1 can tomato paste
2 dried red chili peppers, minced
1 tablespoon minced fresh ginger
4 teaspoons Worcestershire sauce
1 tablespoon honey
6 to 8 dashes Tabasco sauce
Dash of cayenne
Dash of salt
Freshly ground pepper

Melt the butter and oil in a large non-aluminum saucepan. Sauté the onion until translucent, approximately 10 minutes. Add the garlic and sauté a few minutes more. Add the remaining ingredients and mix well. Simmer 30 minutes, stirring occasionally. Marinate chicken or ribs from 1 hour to overnight, as desired.

TERIYAKI SAUCE 1¼ cups

Teriyaki sauce, a favorite Japanese flavor, is perfect for the grill. Try this as a marinade or a basting sauce for chicken or beef.

¼ cup peanut oil
¼ cup soy sauce
½ cup dry red wine
¼ cup rice vinegar or distilled white vinegar
1 whole scallion, coarsely chopped
2 garlic cloves, sliced into rounds
1 teaspoon slivered fresh ginger

Combine all the ingredients in a bowl. Whisk to emulsify. Marinate chicken or beef for 1 hour to overnight before grilling.

COMPOUND BUTTERS   8 tablespoons

Flavored butters can be sliced onto grilled fish, chicken, steaks, lamb, veal, pork, or vegetables. Use any fresh herb in place of the parsley in this recipe, or try mixing in 1 tablespoon of minced garlic, onion, shallot, capers, or pimientos.

> *½ cup butter*
> *Dash of lemon juice*
> *1 tablespoon minced fresh parsley*
> *Salt and pepper to taste*

Allow the butter to soften in a bowl out of the refrigerator until malleable but not melting and oily. With a fork, thoroughly blend in the lemon juice, parsley, and seasonings. On a square sheet of waxed paper, form the butter into a 6-inch log. Using the waxed paper, roll the log into a uniform cylinder. Firm in the refrigerator. Use immediately or store in the freezer, tightly wrapped, indefinitely. Cut off pats as needed.

Herb Butter   Use 1 tablespoon of any minced fresh herb or 1 teaspoon dried herb in place of the parsley. Try basil, rosemary, dill, thyme, mint, tarragon, etc.

Roe or Coral Butter   Add 1 tablespoon fresh lobster coral or tomalley, or your favorite fish roe, pounded to a paste.

Chive Butter   Add 1 tablespoon of minced fresh chives and reduce the amount of parsley to 1 teaspoon.

Anchovy Butter   Add 1 tablespoon anchovy, pounded to a paste.

Horseradish Butter   Add 1 tablespoon prepared horseradish.

AÏOLI   1 cup

This garlic-flavored mayonnaise is an excellent dipping sauce for grilled vegetables. Try Aïoli-Tartar Sauce, below, for fish.

> *3 to 4 garlic cloves*
> *2 egg yolks*
> *1¼ cups olive oil*
> *1 teaspoon Dijon mustard*
> *2 teaspoons fresh lemon juice*
> *Salt and pepper to taste*

Mince the garlic with a little salt until it forms a smooth paste. In a blender, food processor, or with a whisk, beat the garlic and yolks until pale yellow and foamy. Add the oil drop by drop while continuing to beat. When the mixture begins to emulsify, add the oil in a slow, thin stream. When half the oil is gone, add the mustard and alternate oil and lemon juice until both are gone. If the mixture separates, stop and beat until smooth. If the mixture is too thick, add a little more lemon juice. Season with salt and pepper. Aïoli keeps for one week in the refrigerator.

Aïoli-Tartar Sauce   To prepared Aïoli, add 1 tablespoon chopped capers, 2 teaspoons chopped pimientos, 1 tablespoon chopped fresh parsley, and a dash of white wine vinegar. This is excellent with grilled fish, either hot or cold.

PESTO   1½ cups

Some of the most sublime flavors come together in this Italian sauce: fresh sweet basil, pine nuts, olive oil, Parmesan and *pecorino* cheese, and garlic. The result is a smooth sauce that goes well with pasta, fish, veal, and vegetables. Use *only* fresh basil for *pesto*.

> *2 cups fresh basil leaves, firmly packed*
> *½ cup pine nuts*
> *2 or 3 garlic cloves*
> *½ cup freshly grated Parmesan cheese*
>   *(or a mixture of Parmesan and pecorino)*
> *Generous ½ cup olive oil*
> *Salt to taste*

Put all the ingredients in a blender or food processor and blend until smooth, stopping occasionally to scrape down the sides. For a coarser *pesto,* mince the pine nuts and basil leaves and put in a bowl with the olive oil (this keeps the leaves from darkening while you mince the garlic). Mince the garlic and salt together until they form a paste. Add the garlic paste and cheese to the oil and basil mixture and stir well to combine. Store *pesto* with a ¼-inch layer of olive oil over the top in a tightly sealed jar in the refrigerator. Keeps for 6 months.

SALSA   1½ cups

For the spiciest salsa, use *jalapeño* peppers; for milder salsa use canned green chilies or fresh Anaheim or *ancho* chilies. Be careful not to touch your eyes when handling hot chili peppers, and wash your hands immediately after. This thick, chunky salsa goes well with any grilled fish or vegetable.

> *2 large red-ripe or 4 small tomatoes, minced*
> *1 medium-sized onion, minced*
> *2 garlic cloves, minced*
> *Juice of 1 whole lime*
> *Mild: ½ long fresh Anaheim or ancho chili,*
>   *seeded and minced, or 2 canned whole green*
>   *chilies*
> *Spicy: 1 seeded and minced fresh jalapeño*
>   *or 2 canned whole jalapeños*
> *6 or 7 cilantro sprigs*
> *Pinch of sugar*
> *Salt and pepper to taste*

Combine all the ingredients in a bowl and mix well. Allow the salsa to stand at room temperature for 1 hour before serving. Salsa can be made up to 10 days in advance. Store in the refrigerator in a clean glass jar with a tight-fitting lid.

CRÈME FRAÎCHE   1½ cups

The flavor and texture of *crème fraîche* lies somewhere between sour cream and whipped heavy cream. It is smooth, thick, and slightly tart, with a light, refreshing flavor that blends with many different foods and sauces. A dollop on grilled veal or fish melts away leaving a light, almost buttery flavor. Toss it into hot pasta with Parmesan cheese, spoon it over fresh or grilled fruit, or melt it over hot grilled vegetables.

> *½ pint heavy cream*
> *3 tablespoons buttermilk*

Stir the cream and buttermilk together in a clean glass jar with a tight-fitting lid. Put in a warm place to ripen for 6 to 8 hours. Transfer to the refrigerator to chill and thicken. *Crème fraîche* will keep up to 2 weeks in the refrigerator. To make more, repeat the process using 3 tablespoons *crème fraîche* instead of buttermilk.

3 | MEAT, POULTRY & FISH

MEAT

BEEF is perfectly suited for the quick, dry-heat cooking of the grill, which keeps it tender and juicy inside, and gives it a delicious charcoal flavor on the outside.

Select cuts labeled "Prime" or "Choice" for grilling. These are from the highest-quality beef and will have the most flavor and best texture. Look for bright-red firm flesh. Beef should not be dark or dried-out looking. Buy steaks at least 1 inch thick. Marbling provides an internal basting liquid, so choose cuts with a fair amount of it. The fat surrounding the meat should be creamy white. Don't trim all of this fat off, as it will hold in juices while the meat cooks. Store beef in the refrigerator in the butcher paper or loosely wrapped in waxed paper, but always bring it to room temperature before grilling. Never salt beef before grilling it; salt draws out the juices that keep the meat tender.

Steaks

The best steaks come from the loin section of the cow. This is one of its least-used muscles, so the meat it yields is the most tender. The loin contains a large portion of the tenderloin, a long muscle highly prized for its smoothness, tenderness, and rich flavor. A typical loin steak will contain some of the tenderloin; the more it has, the more tender the steak will be. The porterhouse and T-bone are about half loin, half tenderloin meat, and are generally considered to be the best steaks. Other loin steaks, variously called the New York strip, club, and Kansas City strip (to name a few) are also quite delicious. Steaks cut entirely from the tenderloin are the filet mignon, Chateaubriand, and tournedos. Though they tend to be pricey, these steaks are excellent grilled.

How To Cook Steaks   Always bring steaks to room temperature before grilling. Slit the fat surrounding the meat in a few places to keep steaks from curling on the grill, but do not pierce the meat. Rub the hot cooking rack with a small piece of fat, or brush it with oil. Sear steaks on both sides for 30 seconds each, with the cover off. Grill steaks according to the recommended times listed below, turning only once after searing, over a medium-hot fire on an open grill (although for steaks thicker than 1½ inches we suggest you cover the grill). Don't prick the meat with a fork, as this releases juices.

To check for doneness, make a small cut near the bone to see if it is cooked to your liking. We suggest you check it just *before* intuition tells you it's done. If not, it can *always* go back on the grill.

The entire tenderloin muscle can be grilled whole and sliced into thick steaks after grilling. Grill it covered over medium-hot coals for 12 minutes per side for rare, 14 for medium-rare, 16 for medium. Check the meat by making a small cut into the thickest part.

Steaks/Minutes Per Side

Thickness	Rare	Medium-rare	Medium	Well-done
1 inch	3	4	5	6
1½ inches	4–5	5–6	6–7	8–9
2 inches	6–7	7–8	8–9	9–10

Sirloin   Sirloin steaks are cut from the slightly less-tender section of the loin, but are fine for the grill. They may be further tenderized by a red wine marinade, if desired. Grill sirloin steaks according to the preceding chart.

Round   Most round steaks are not tender enough for dry heat cooking. However, the steak off the top of the round is a fairly tender cut for grilling, especially if marinated. This cut is variously labeled London Broil, Butterball, or simply Top Round Steak. Grill it according to the preceding chart. Suggested marinades: Red Wine Marinade, Sesame Marinade, Asian Barbecue Marinade.

Rib   The rib, which lies near the loin section, is also naturally tender. The best rib steak is the rib-eye or Delmonico, which contains some of the tenderloin muscle. Cook these steaks according to the preceding chart.

The whole rib roast can be cooked slowly on a covered grill. Use indirect heat with a drip pan positioned on the fuel grate under the meat (for an explanation of indirect cooking, see page 28). Cook the rib roast 10 to 15 minutes per pound, or until a meat thermometer registers 140° for rare, 150° for medium-rare, and 160° for medium.

Marinate beef back ribs overnight, bake in an oven at 350° for 45 minutes, and grill covered over a medium-hot fire for 15 to 20 minutes.

Flank   This long, sinewy muscle is delicious if marinated up to 48 hours and cooked very quickly on an open grill. Grill flat over a red-hot to medium-hot fire for 6 to 7 minutes per side. To carve, position a sharp knife almost flat against the top of the meat and slice off very thin oval slices, cutting diagonally across the grain. Suggested marinades: any red wine marinade; Sesame Marinade; Sherry Vinegar, Port, and Prune Marinade; Asian Barbecue Marinade.

Hamburgers   Select ground beef or chuck that is bright red with some fat for juicy burgers. Handle the meat as little as possible when shaping it into patties, as this breaks up the fat and may cause the burgers to dry out on the grill. Grill a 1½-inch burger on an open grill over a medium-hot fire for 4 to 5 minutes per side for medium-rare.

VEAL

Most American veal is from calves 8 to 12 weeks old. It will be labeled "milk-fed" or "dairy," although most calves have been weaned and have even been allowed to graze a bit. The more the calf has grazed, the more pinkish in color the veal will be due to the iron content in the grass. It will, though, be quite tender and very low in fat.

The rib and loin chop cuts of veal are the tenderest and best suited for the grill. Because veal is low in fat, cook it quickly on an open grill over a medium-hot fire, for approximately 6 minutes per side for a 1½-inch chop.

Suggested marinades: any white or red wine marinade; Lemon Marinade.

LAMB

The tenderest cuts of lamb come from the loin and rib. Grill chops on an open grill over a medium-hot fire for 4 to 5 minutes per side for a 1½-inch chop.

Leg of lamb is also quite tender, and it is very flavorful. Grill it unboned on a covered grill using indirect heat, over a medium-hot fire. Cook approximately 20 to 25 minutes per pound, until the internal temperature is 135° for rare and 145° for medium. Replenish the coals every 45 minutes or so. Allow the roast to sit for 15 minutes before carving. Leg of lamb is also delicious butterflied (the bone removed and the meat spread out flat; have your butcher do this for you). The differing thicknesses in the flat piece will yield slices of every degree of doneness—something for everyone. Cook on an open grill over a medium-hot fire for 15 to 20 minutes per side. Lamb is delicious after marinating overnight, which tenderizes it and gives it flavor.

The rack of lamb can be grilled for flavorful, thick rib chops. Have the chine bone between the ribs cracked so that carving will be easier. On a covered grill over a medium-hot fire,

cook 20 minutes, fat side down. Turn, then cook another 25 to 30 minutes.

Suggested marinades: any red wine marinade; Zinfandel Sauce.

PORK

Pork loin chops, particularly the "center cuts," are the tenderest for the grill. Sear a 1½-inch chop on an open grill over a medium-hot fire 1 minute per side. Cover and cook another 6 to 7 minutes per side.

Boned pork loin roasts are excellent marinated and grilled. On an open grill, sear a 1½-pound boned and rolled roast (serves 4) over a medium-hot fire for 10 minutes per side. Cover the grill and continue cooking another 30 to 40 minutes, to 140° (most cookbooks recommend 170°, which is overcooked in our opinion).

Pork ribs are a grilling classic. The meatiest ribs from the back are called "country-style" ribs, and are generally marketed as individual ribs. Slightly less meaty but just as tender and flavorful are baby back ribs, which are sold in racks. Spareribs are cut from the side of the pig, and are delicious marinated overnight and grilled. Bake marinated ribs in a 350° oven for 40 minutes. Grill on a closed grill over a medium-hot fire for 10 to 15 minutes per side.

Suggested marinades: any red wine marinade; Sherry Vinegar, Port, and Prune Marinade; Honey, Tamari, and Orange Marinade; Asian Barbecue Marinade; Traditional or Spicy Barbecue Sauce.

VARIETY MEATS

Liver Calves' liver has the best texture and flavor, and is delicious grilled. Brush ½-inch liver slices with oil. On an open grill over a medium-hot to red-hot fire, grill liver approximately 1 to 2 minutes per side. Avoid overcooking liver as it becomes dry. Squeeze a little lemon juice on cooked liver and serve.

Sweetbreads Sweetbreads are the thymus gland or pancreas from beef, veal, or lamb, but the tenderest are from veal and lamb. All sweetbreads require some advance preparation before grilling, but they are well worth the

Testing for doneness

effort. Their delicious, subtle flavor will convert even the squeamish. Soak sweetbreads in cold water with a squeeze of lemon juice in the refrigerator for 1½ hours, changing the water two or three times. In a saucepan, bring the sweetbreads to a gentle boil in fresh water, reduce the heat, and simmer gently for 10 minutes. Plunge them into cold water and pull away the whitish membrane (this membrane is tough, and will cause them to curl on the grill). Place the sweetbreads between several layers of paper towels and flatten them under a weight for an hour or so. Brush with oil. On an open grill over a medium-hot fire, grill 4 to 5 minutes per side. Squeeze a little lemon juice over the grilled sweetbreads and serve with a lemon wedge.

Kidneys   Buy tender veal or lamb kidneys for the grill. Soak in cold water with a dash of lemon juice for an hour or so. Split each kidney lengthwise down the middle and remove the fat and membrane. Brush with oil. On an open grill over a medium-hot fire, grill approximately 10 to 15 minutes, turning frequently to brown all sides. Kidney should be pink in the middle. Squeeze a little lemon juice over the grilled kidneys and serve.

SAUSAGES

Sausages are delicious grilled. They become crispy and brown on the outside and juicy inside, while absorbing the smoky flavor of the grill. There are dozens of sausage types, made from pork, beef, lamb, or veal, or a combination of these. Italian hot and mild, French wine, garlic, bratwurst, bockwurst, knockwurst, kielbasa, Louisiana hots, and *linguiça* are only a few of the available sausage varieties.

To grill, separate linked sausages. Prick the skins in a few places to allow the fat to run out. Cook sausages on a covered grill over a medium-hot fire. Grease drips from sausages as they cook, which causes flare-ups if the fire is too hot. Close down the vents to cool the fire a bit if this happens. As a general guideline, grill 1-inch-diameter sausages for 8 minutes; 10 to 12 minutes for 1½- to 2-inch-diameter sausages. Turn the sausages frequently to brown all sides evenly. To check doneness, cut into one sausage. If the middle is still pink, cook a little longer.

CHICKEN

Chicken is a versatile meat that can be grilled whole, split, quartered, cut into parts, or boned. Its mild flavor absorbs the good grill smoke, and it combines well with many different marinades. Look for fresh plump chickens with pale-white skin. Buy only young chickens, which will be labeled "Broiler," "Roaster," or "Fryer," depending on the weight of the bird.

Cook chicken on a covered grill, as its skin is fatty and tends to cause flare-ups. Cooking it covered also helps keep it moist and evenly browned. If you are using an open grill, allow the coals to reach the medium-hot to slow stage before cooking to minimize flare-ups, and grill it as far from the fire as possible.

To cook whole birds, salt and pepper the cavity and rub the skin with oil or baste. Use indirect heat and place a drip pan on the fuel grate under the chicken to collect drippings. Place the bird in a roasting rack (optional, but more convenient) and grill covered, breast down, for 20 minutes. Baste every 10 minutes. Turn breast up and finish cooking. Whole chickens require 15 to 20 minutes per pound. To test, prick the thigh meat near the bone. If the juices run clear and the leg feels slightly loose, the chicken is done.

Chicken pieces cook faster than whole chickens. To cook, start chicken pieces skin-side down directly over medium-hot coals. Grill, covered, for 15 minutes. Turn and grill 15 to 20 minutes more, until the juices run clear.

Boned chicken can easily be overcooked, which makes it dry. Grill boned chicken pieces approximately 4 to 6 minutes per side over medium-hot coals. If the chicken is skinned, the grill does not need to be covered.

Poussins are baby chickens, which weigh in at under a pound. They are tasty grilled whole or split, for approximately 20 to 30 minutes total, depending on the size. Grill, covered, over medium-hot coals.

Capons are castrated roosters that have been allowed to fatten. They are generally quite flavorful, and can be cooked like whole chickens, gauging the cooking time by weight.

Suggested marinades: any white wine marinade; Peanut Marinade; Raspberry Vinegar Marinade; Mustard Marinade; Lemon Marinade; Lime Marinade; any barbecue sauce. Chicken combines well with almost any marinade.

ROCK CORNISH GAME HENS

These small, tasty birds are not wild game hens at all, but rather are the offspring of the Plymouth Rock hen and the Cornish game cock. The result is a tender, juicy bird of all-white meat. Cook whole or butterflied. Whole hens cook on a covered grill over medium-hot coals for 30 minutes or until the juices run clear. Baste every 5 minutes to add moisture as they cook.

To butterfly hens, slice all the way down one side of the backbone and open out flat. Cut along the other side of the backbone and discard the bone. Place each hen skin-side up on a board, and flatten by pressing firmly on the breastbone. It will crack a little and flatten out. To split whole hens, simply slice the birds vertically right down the middle into 2 equal halves. Brush with oil and sear butterflied or split hens on an open grill for 1 to 2 minutes per side. Grill, covered, for a total of 20 minutes, turning several times and basting while cooking.

Suggested marinades: any white wine marinade; Lemon Marinade; Raspberry Vinegar Marinade.

DUCK

Fresh duck is rich and flavorful, one of the great culinary luxuries. Most ducks available in the United States are raised domestically, now primarily in Indiana and Wisconsin (despite the name "Long Island" duck, which refers to where the first imported Chinese White Pekin ducks were raised).

Duck is delicious grilled, but it must be cooked carefully. It is fatty, and its dripping causes flare-ups that can be disastrous to gorgeous, fresh duck. For this reason we opt for boned duck breasts, which cook more quickly than whole ducks. Before grilling, remove any chunks of fat. Rinse and pat dry, and prick the skin (not the flesh) to let some of the fat run out while it cooks. To further decrease flare-ups, use indirect heat with a drip pan placed on the fuel grate under the duck.

Sear the duck 2 minutes per side over medium-hot coals. Cover the grill and continue cooking 10 minutes per side. Cut into the duck to check doneness. The flesh should be pink and juicy.

Suggested marinades: any red or white wine marinade; Raspberry Vinegar Marinade; Tarragon Marinade; Honey, Tamari, and Orange Marinade.

GAME BIRDS

Game hens, squab, quail, and pheasant are tasty grilled. Grill small birds whole or butterflied on a covered grill over medium-hot coals. Most birds require 15 to 30 minutes total, depending on size. Baste every 5 minutes to add moisture. To test doneness, either cut into the flesh or prick the skin to see if the juices run clear. Avoid overcooking game birds, which makes the flesh dry and stringy.

Suggested marinades: any red or white wine marinade; Raspberry Vinegar Marinade; Tarragon Marinade.

TURKEY

Turkey is delicious cooked with slow, moist heat on a covered grill. Avoid frozen turkeys, which tend to dry out when cooked. "Self-basting" turkeys are also lacking in flavor. If desired, you may stuff a turkey for the grill, which also helps to hold in moisture.

Duck, pheasant, and poussin

*Pork ribs in Honey, Tamari,
and Orange Marinade*

Cook turkey over a slow, indirect fire. Place a
drip pan half filled with wine, broth, or water
on the fuel grate under the bird to create steam
inside the grill. Cook the turkey on a roasting
rack, starting with the breast side down, on a
covered grill, for 13 to 15 minutes per pound.
Baste the turkey every 15 to 20 minutes. Turn
breast up halfway through cooking. Replenish
the coals every 45 minutes as the turkey cooks
(add either hot coals that you have started in a
chimney or new coals, making sure they touch
the live coals to ignite). Cook the bird until a
meat thermometer inserted in the breast
reads 170°.

FISH

Fish is naturally delicious on the grill, and perfectly suited to simple, straightforward dry-heat cooking. Fish is self-basting, and if correctly cooked it will be tender, juicy, and succulent. Even better, fish is quite low in cholesterol and fat, and it can be grilled with very little extra fat or oil, if desired. It absorbs the smoky flavors of the grill even though it cooks quickly and retains a very fresh flavor and light texture.

The most important rule to remember for fish is not to overcook it! Fish can go from perfectly cooked to overcooked very quickly. As a general rule, a ¾-inch fish fillet cooks in approximately 8 minutes total, and a 1-inch fish steak will cook in 10 minutes or less. Bring fish to room temperature before grilling so it will cook evenly.

Lean fish such as swordfish, sea bass, and rockfish will benefit from a half-hour oil marinade to keep it from drying out on the grill. Most fish, however, contains enough natural oil to keep it juicy, and needs only a light brushing with oil or butter to prevent it from sticking to the grill. Wine, vinegar, and especially lemon or lime juice will "cook" fish, so use it sparingly in fish marinades.

Always oil the cooking rack before grilling fish. Cook fish 1½ inches thick and under on an open grill over a red-hot fire. This cooks it quickly and sears in juices. Grill thicker fish on a covered grill to keep the outside from overcooking before the inside is done. Move fish as little as possible to keep it from breaking up, and turn it only once during cooking. A long-bladed spatula is best for this job, as the whole fish, steak, or fillet will slide onto it without breaking. An oiled hinged fish basket is also excellent for grilling large fish fillets and whole fish.

Fish is naturally formed in layers that become easier to separate as it cooks. When these layers, or flakes, come apart relatively easily and the flesh in the center is barely opaque, the fish is done. Fish becomes firmer when done but it should not be hard, and it should remain juicy.

Prawns, lobster, and crab cook quickly on the grill and are done when the flesh turns from translucent to opaque. Shellfish, such as oysters and clams, if cooked whole in the shell, is done when the shell pops open; if shelled and skewered it is done in less than 5 minutes, when the flesh is firm.

SHELLFISH

Abalone   Abalone is found along the California coast, though it gets more scarce each year. If you find fresh abalone steaks, by all means try them.

Pound steaks with a wooden mallet until about ¼ inch thick. This requires some dedication, but don't give up. Brush pounded steaks with oil or butter and grill on an open grill over a *very* red-hot fire for no more than about 15 to 20 seconds per side.

Suggested sauces: Lemon Butter Sauce; Salsa.

Clams   Clams live in the waters of both coasts, but they are particularly abundant on the East Coast. Steamers, quahogs, littlenecks, and cherrystones all come from Atlantic waters, though the Pacific boasts the razor, Pismo, and Pacific littleneck. Like oysters, clams poach in their own shells on the grill, and pop wide open when cooked.

Select fresh clams that close up tightly when tapped. Clams should feel slightly heavy and their shells should be intact. Scrub the shells and soak in several changes of salted water for an hour. This encourages clams to spit out sand and grit. Place clams on an open grill over a red-hot fire, and remove when the shells pop wide open, approximately 3 to 5 minutes. Discard any that do not open.

Suggested sauces: White Wine Butter Sauce; Lemon Butter Sauce; Salsa; Aïoli.

Crab   Crab comes from the East Coast (rock, stone, and blue crab), the West Coast (Dungeness), and Alaska (king crab). Select the largest, liveliest, freshest crabs for grilling. To kill a live crab, drop it in boiling water for 2 minutes. Remove and run it under cold water. Holding the legs, pull off the top shell and discard. Turn the crab over and remove the breastplate by pulling the triangular piece of shell. Turn the crab back over and pull off the gray feathery gills along the sides. Remove the white intestine and grayish matter along the back, pull out the mouth parts, and discard. Reserve the green tomalley and any orange roe for flavoring compound butters or butter sauces. Carefully rinse away the remaining matter and cut the crab in half down the middle. Crack the claws and legs and marinate the crab halves or brush with oil or butter. On an open grill over a red-hot fire, grill crab halves 3 to 4 minutes per side, until the shell is bright red and the exposed flesh is opaque.

Suggested marinades and sauces: any oil marinade; White Wine Butter Sauce; Lemon Butter Sauce; Compound Butter.

Lobster   Buy live lobster and kill it before grilling by inserting a sharp knife crosswise where the head meets the shell to sever the spinal cord (there is no need to remove the head). Turn the lobster on its back, make a deep cut down the length of the body without cutting through the shell, and open it out. Remove the black vein and stomach (near the head). Remove and save the green tomalley and orange roe or coral for compound butters. Crack the claws and brush the flesh with olive oil or butter. On an open grill over red-hot coals, grill whole lobster flesh-side down for 6 to 8 minutes. Turn, baste, and cook another

minute or two. Lobster is done when the flesh is just opaque and the shell is bright red.

Lobster tail, often taken from the spiny lobster (because it lacks meaty front claws), is quick and easy. Grill it as you would whole lobster, for 3 to 5 minutes per side.

Suggested marinades and sauces: any white wine marinade; Nam Prik Marinade; White Wine Butter Sauce; Lemon Butter Sauce; Coral or Tomalley Butter.

Mussels   Mussels can be tossed on the grill in the shell to poach in their own liquid. Buy mussels when they are in season, which is all year on the East Coast, and November through April in the West. Mussels should close tightly when rapped or handled, and they should feel slightly heavy in the hand. Scrub the shells. With a firm tug, pull out the "beard" (the grassy fibers hanging out of the shell). Toss on an open grill over red-hot coals until they open, approximately 5 to 7 minutes.

Suggested sauces: White Wine Butter Sauce; Salsa; Aïoli; Crème Fraîche.

Oysters   There are dozens of oyster varieties, the most well known of which are the Tomales Bay (Pacific), bluepoint (Atlantic), and Walapa (Pacific Northwest). Lightly cooked on the grill, oysters are a delicious treat. They poach right in their own shells and open when ready. Try them as appetizers while waiting for the coals to burn down before grilling the main course.

Select fresh oysters with tightly closed shells. Scrub the shells under running water. Store loosely wrapped in a paper bag or in a bowl in the refrigerator until needed. Bring to room temperature before grilling. Put the whole shells on an open grill over a red-hot fire, with the flat side of the shell up. Oysters will open very slightly after 5 to 6 minutes. Discard any shells that do not open. Remove with tongs and, holding with a mitt, flat side up, pull off the top shell. If the oyster is still attached to the top shell, scrape it off into the bottom shell, being careful to retain the juices or "liquor" in the bottom shell. Serve as is, or add sauce to the bottom shell and simmer again briefly on the grill.

Cod, mussels, clams, crayfish, and scallops

Suggested sauces: White Wine Butter Sauce; Lemon Butter Sauce; Salsa; Barbecue Sauce. Try sprinkling on a little grated cheese as well.

Scallops   Tender, succulent scallops are delicious grilled. We like the large sea scallops for the grill, though the small bay scallops can be skewered and quickly grilled. Skewer scallops, brush with oil or butter, and grill on an open grill over a red-hot fire, turning frequently to cook all sides. Scallops are done when they just turn opaque, approximately 4 to 6 minutes for the larger ones.

Shrimp and Prawns   For grilling we recommend medium to jumbo shrimp. Also called prawns, jumbo shrimp are large and meaty and come in a variety of colors. Some, like striped tiger shrimp, are quite spectacular. Buy only fresh shrimp, and look for firm, translucent flesh, avoiding those with loose shells. Grill shrimp either shelled or in the shell. To shell, begin on the underside at the head end. Separate the shell and gently pull it away, working your way down toward the tail. The shell should pull off easily. Remove the dark vein that runs down the back just under the surface of the flesh with a paring knife. Brush shrimp with a little oil or butter before grilling, or marinate. Grill it skewered over a red-hot fire on an open grill. Shrimp are done when the flesh has just turned opaque and firm, 2 to 3 minutes per side.

Suggested marinades: any white wine marinade; Nam Prik Marinade; White Wine Butter Sauce.

Squid   Squid cooks extremely quickly on a hot grill, making it a wonderful snack while waiting for the coals to burn down. The long, cylindrical body can be grilled whole or opened out flat, or it can be cut into rings and skewered with the tentacles. Buy squid cleaned or whole. To clean, cut off the tentacles just below the eye, leaving the eye on the body. Squeeze out the conical beak from the opening of the tentacles. Press down firmly at the head to pull it off the body, and discard it. Rinse the inky entrails out of the body and pull out the hard quill visible just inside. Rinse again and pat dry. Brush with oil or butter and grill whole or

skewered (the tentacles must be skewered, as they will fall through the cooking rack) on an open grill over a red-hot fire. Squid will cook in minutes, and is done when it curls and is barely opaque.

FRESH AND SALTWATER FISH

Angler or Monkfish   This fascinating fish is found along the New England coast. It gets its name from the long spine attached to its large head, with which it "angles" for its dinners of small fish and shellfish. Its firm, dense, sweet flesh tastes very much like lobster, and it is delicious grilled.

Buy thin fillets, brush with oil or butter, and grill quickly over red-hot coals on an open grill.

Suggested marinades and sauces: any oil marinade; any simple butter sauce; Red Pepper Butter Sauce.

Cod   Another lean mild white-fleshed fish, cod is available year round on both coasts, though primarily on the Atlantic. It is usually sold as fillets or steaks.

Cod tends to get dry on the grill, and benefits from an oil marinade or a butter baste. Grill over a medium-hot to red-hot fire on an open grill.

Suggested marinades and sauces: any oil marinade; any simple butter sauce; Red Pepper Butter Sauce; Aïoli; Aïoli-Tartar Sauce; Compound Butter; Crème Fraîche.

Flounder   Flounder is very similar to sole and is in fact often marketed as lemon or gray sole. It is a flatfish, with fine-textured white flesh. It is widely available on both coasts and is generally sold as fillets.

Cook lightly oiled fillets on an open grill over red-hot coals.

Suggested sauces: any simple butter sauce; Lemon Butter Sauce; Compound Butter; Aïoli; Aïoli-Tartar Sauce.

Grouper   The category of *grouper* includes a great many species of fish. All are medium-rich, slightly oily fish, with firm white flesh and good flavor. This fish is available everywhere, year round, and is usually sold as steaks or fillets.

Cook on an open grill over medium-hot to red-hot coals.

Suggested marinades and sauces: any oil marinade; any simple butter sauce; Red Pepper Butter Sauce; Compound Butter; Aïoli-Tartar Sauce.

Halibut   Halibut, like sole, is a flatfish and a bottom-dweller, but it tends to be much larger than sole. It has firm fine-textured flesh that is slightly sweet, and is usually sold as steaks. Brush with oil and grill over a red-hot fire on an open grill.

Suggested marinades and sauces: any oil marinade; any simple butter sauce; Compound Butter; Crème Fraîche; Aïoli.

Mackerel   Very fresh mackerel can be delicious grilled whole and butterflied (dressed, head and tail removed, and spread out flat). The skin becomes crispy, and the strong-flavored flesh absorbs the smoky grill flavors.

Mackerel is oily, so it will not need oil or a marinade. Start it flesh-side down on an open grill over medium-hot to red-hot coals. Turn flesh-side up and finish. Remove it carefully, as the skin tends to stick to the grill.

Red Snapper   This very popular lean fish lives in both Atlantic and Pacific waters and boasts over 250 species. It is known for its light pinkish flesh, which has a mild, almost sweet flavor.

Snapper fillets hold together quite well on the grill. Brush with oil and grill over a red-hot to medium-hot fire on an open grill.

Suggested marinades and sauces: any oil marinade; Compound Butter; Red Pepper Butter Sauce; Aïoli; Pesto.

Rockfish   Called tilefish on the East Coast, this lean mild white-fleshed fish is widely available. It combines well with many marinades and sauces, but needs at least an oil or butter baste on the grill. It is sold as fillets, and should be grilled on an open grill over medium-hot to red-hot coals.

Suggested marinades and sauces: any oil marinade; any simple butter sauce; Compound Butter; Red Pepper Butter Sauce; Aïoli; Aïoli-Tartar Sauce.

Salmon   This pink-fleshed, fine-textured fish is a favorite for the grill. During the summer months, salmon is available on both coasts (the Atlantic salmon starts a bit earlier, in June), but most fresh salmon comes from Washington state. It is generally sold as steaks, or whole if small. Its oily flesh keeps it moist, and it absorbs flavorful smoke. When cooked correctly, salmon is one of the most luxurious and delicious fish to come off the grill.

Brush with oil or marinate briefly in a white wine or oil marinade, and grill on an open grill over red-hot to medium-hot coals.

Suggested marinades and sauces: White Wine Marinade (decrease the amount of wine and vinegar); Red Pepper Butter Sauce; White Wine Butter Sauce; Lemon Butter Sauce; Compound Butter; Crème Fraîche.

Sea Bass   Sea bass is a Pacific Ocean fish very similar to grouper. It is commonly sold in steaks and fillets, and its season is spring and summer.

Cook sea bass the same way you would grouper. It is a lean fish and benefits from an oil marinade.

Suggested marinades and sauces: any oil marinade; any simple butter sauce; Aïoli; Aïoli-Tartar Sauce.

Shark   In recent years, shark has enjoyed new recognition for its food value, mild flavor, and lean flesh. Its firm texture is suited for the grill, though it tends to dry out if overcooked. Shark naturally develops a slight ammonia odor and should be soaked for 30 minutes in mildly acidic water (add lemon juice or vinegar) or milk to neutralize the odor.

Shark is commonly sold as fillets and steaks. Rub them with oil and grill quickly over red-hot coals on an open grill.

Sole   Sole is a moist flavorful flatfish that is excellent grilled. It has fine-textured white flesh that absorbs grill flavors and combines well with many sauces. The Pacific varieties are petrale, rex, and English, while the Atlantic variety, Dover sole, is found only off the shores of England.

Sole is usually sold whole (dressed) and as fillets. Brush with oil and grill over medium-hot to red-hot coals on an open grill.

Suggested sauces: any simple butter sauce; Red Pepper Butter Sauce.

Swordfish   This big deep-sea fish is quite popular for the grill. It is available year round on both coasts, though the height of its season is summer and fall. Swordfish has firm, fine-textured white flesh with an almost beefy flavor, and is most commonly sold as steaks.

Swordfish is lean and should be marinated or brushed with plenty of oil before grilling. Grill on an open grill over medium-hot to red-hot coals.

Suggested marinades and sauces: Nam Prik Marinade; any oil marinade; White Wine Butter Sauce; Red Pepper Butter Sauce.

Trout   Trout is available year round, as most of it, including the ever-present rainbow trout, is grown on farms. Unfortunately, it lacks the flavor of its wild brook relatives such as the brook trout, brown trout, steelhead, cutthroat, or lake trout. Fishermen claim that the harder the life of the trout, the more flavor it will have (an idea born, no doubt, of their time-honored struggle with this elusive mountain-stream prey).

Avoid frozen trout. It is almost completely lacking in flavor. Pick out a stiff fresh fish with clear eyes, preferably one that has been dressed (gutted but still whole). Brush with oil and grill on an open grill over red-hot to medium-hot coals for approximately 5 to 7 minutes per side, or until the flesh turns opaque.

Suggested marinades and sauces: any oil marinade; Compound Butter; any simple butter sauce.

Tuna   Tuna is a mild saltwater fish available year round on both coasts. Its deep-red flesh turns white when cooked.

Both steaks and fillets are good for the grill. Oil the fish and cook on an open grill over medium-hot coals.

Suggested marinades and sauces: any oil marinade; Compound Butter; Red Pepper Butter Sauce; Aïoli.

4 | VEGETABLES & FRUIT

VEGETABLES

VEGETABLES are often overlooked for the grill, and the time to correct this oversight has arrived. Grilling vegetables heightens their own natural flavor, while giving them a light smoky grill flavor.

The dry intense heat of the coals quickly seals the outside of vegetables, allowing the flesh to cook in its own natural moisture. If first boiled and then grilled, vegetables lose flavor and tend to be a bit mushy. Avoid peeling vegetables for the grill—not only for aesthetic reasons, but also because the skins become quite crispy and delicious.

Brush vegetable skins and flesh with oil before grilling. Vegetables are easy to grill and will cook beautifully over any temperature of fire. If they are overcooking on the outside, simply move the vegetables away from the hottest part of the fire. We like to start vegetables over the hot coals to sear their skins, and then move them to the sides of the grill while the main course is grilled. Most vegetables require 15 to 20 minutes on a covered grill, and 5 to 10 minutes longer on an open grill. To check doneness, poke with a skewer: if it goes in easily the vegetables are done.

Hinged grills are useful for cooking vegetables that tend to fall apart on the grill, such as tomato and onion slices.

ARTICHOKES

Baby artichokes, artichoke hearts, or quarters are delicious grilled. They are, however, the exception to the rule that vegetables need not be steamed beforehand. Raw artichokes will not cook through on the grill, and must be steamed and pared before grilling. For large artichokes, rinse thoroughly and trim the stalk to ½ inch. Make 2 or 3 small slits in the stalk end with the tip of a knife so the heart will cook more quickly. Steam 30 to 45 minutes in a covered kettle. Artichokes are done when a leaf near the bottom pulls away easily. Remove, cut into quarters, pull out the choke, and grill. For hearts, pull off all the leaves and the choke. Grill the whole heart or cut it into pieces, brush with oil, skewer, and grill. Steam small artichokes whole, skewer, and grill. Artichokes should be done when you put them on the grill, so you can then grill them to your desired brownness.

CARROTS

Carrots become slightly crisp on the outside and fluffy and light on the inside when grilled. Pick out the freshest medium-sized carrots. The freshest are those with the green tops still on; break these off before grilling. If these are unavailable, select bright-orange carrots, avoiding those with a dull color and cracks. Scrub under cold running water and pat dry. Do not peel. Rub with oil and grill whole, turning frequently, until tender when pierced with a skewer, approximately 20 to 25 minutes.

CORN

Fresh tender corn on the cob, grilled in the husk, must certainly be one of the most beautiful vegetables on the grill: bright yellow rows of corn peek out from behind the pale green husks with their dark brown grill marks. The corn steams in its own husk, which adds a faint flavor.

Select corn with the whole husk and silk (the tops should not be lopped off). Peek inside at the top to make sure the kernels are plump and even. To prepare corn for the grill, *gently* pull the husk down (as if you are peeling a banana), working your way around the ear. Try to avoid breaking the husk off at the base. Stop about 2 inches from the base. Remove as much silk as possible. Pull the husk back up over the corn and tie the top securely, making a knot with a thin piece of husk (or string). Soak in water for 10 to 15 minutes. Squeeze out the excess water and grill, turning occasionally, for 15 to 20 minutes. Peel off the husks and eat.

EGGPLANT

We think eggplant is at its best on the grill. Its spongy flesh absorbs the flavorful grill smoke, and its full flavor is brought out by the dry heat cooking.

The two most common eggplant varieties are the large rounded types and the long narrow Japanese variety that looks somewhat like a purple zucchini. On all eggplant, look for tight dark-purple skin with no mottling, soft spots, or withering.

Slice large eggplant into ½-inch rounds. To eliminate any bitterness, salt slices on both sides and spread them in one layer on paper towels. Allow them to drain for 30 minutes. Dab the tops with paper towels, pressing slightly to squeeze out some of the moisture. Brush lightly with oil and grill 7 minutes per side over medium-hot coals, or until tender when poked with a skewer.

Slice Japanese eggplant in half lengthwise. This variety is not bitter, so it will not need to be salted and drained. Brush the halves with oil and grill over medium-hot coals for 5 minutes per side. Small Japanese eggplants can be grilled whole, if desired.

GARLIC

When baked through, garlic becomes a mild, almost nutty paste that is delicious squeezed onto bread.

Select firm, evenly formed heads of garlic. Peel away some of the papery layers, particularly from down among the top cloves on the head, but do not pierce or expose the cloves. From a piece of heavy aluminum foil form a muffin-sized leakproof cup, or use a small muffin or pie tin. Place the garlic in the cup and drizzle 1 tablespoon of olive oil over the top, allowing it to run down in between the cloves and into the bottom of the cup. Sprinkle with salt, pepper, and a little thyme, rosemary, or sage. Place on the grill, away from the hottest spot. Cover and cook 35 to 40 minutes. Drizzle twice during cooking with ½ tablespoon of oil. Cover and cook 10 to 15 minutes more, or until the cloves feel quite mushy. To serve, place the whole head on a plate and pour the olive oil it has cooked in over it. Pull off 1 clove at a time and squeeze the paste out the bottom of the clove onto bread (dip the bread in the olive oil, if desired).

LEEKS

Leeks have a mild oniony flavor that goes well with grilled food. Look for small leeks with vibrant green tops. To remove the grit, slice from the top down the middle of the leek to within 2 inches of the base. Rinse well to remove the grit from between the layers. Trim off the roots. Slice very large leeks in half lengthwise, trim the roots, rinse, and secure the layers with dampened toothpicks. Rub with oil or marinate briefly in a little oil and white wine vinegar. Grill whole small or halved leeks until browned and tender, approximately 10 to 15 minutes.

MUSHROOMS

The white round cultivated mushroom is ubiquitous in grocery store produce sections. Though it tends to be watery and a little flavorless, grilling steams out the moisture, leaving a firmer, tastier mushroom. Shiitakes are excellent for the grill, and are becoming more widely available. They have a rich, meaty flavor and firm texture. Cèpes (or *porcini*) mushrooms are also good grilled. Any dried mushrooms should be soaked in warm water for at least 30 minutes before grilling. Skewer mushrooms alone or with other vegetables, meats, seafood, or poultry and grill until browned and tender.

ONIONS

Any type of onion is perfect for the grill. Whole scallions can be skillfully maneuvered on the grill so not one falls through. Larger Spanish or red onions, yellow or white onions, sweet Vidalias and Walla Wallas, torpedoes, and tiny pearl onions can be grilled. Quarter larger onions or slice into rounds. Grill smaller onions whole. Do not parboil onions, as they become mushy. Brush onion quarters with oil and skewer in two places to hold the layers together. For rounds, try skewering the onion before slicing, and then carefully slice between the sticks. Brush with oil. Grill onion quarters and slices for 10 to 20 minutes, or until glossy brown and tender when pierced with a skewer.

Rub scallions with oil and grill, turning frequently, for 10 minutes, or until brown and tender. Leave the green tops on for decoration.

Peel small onions and grill whole, skewered, for 20 to 30 minutes over medium-hot coals on a covered grill.

PEPPERS

While you are watching the flaming coals burn down to the perfect medium-hot fire for your steak or chop, toss a whole pepper on the grill to have later on a salad or pasta. Char the skin of any red, green, or yellow bell pepper until black and crackly all over. When completely charred, place the peppers in a closed paper bag to steam for 10 to 15 minutes. Peel away the charred skin or gently scrape it off with a fork or dull knife. Cut off the tops and remove the seeds. Do not rinse. Slice lengthwise into ¾-inch-wide strips and marinate in olive oil and cracked pepper for 30 minutes. Peppers will keep in the refrigerator for several weeks. Cook hot peppers the same way. When peeling, do not touch your eyes, and always wash your hands afterwards. The milder hot peppers, such as the *ancho,* the *Anaheim,* or the long green *poblano,* can be cooked the same way, and their milder flavors complement less spicy foods. Peppers can also be grilled without charring or peeling. Cook skewered slices, rings, quarters, or whole peppers over a medium-hot fire, turning frequently, until brown and tender.

POTATOES

Potatoes cook beautifully on the grill. They become golden brown on the outside while the inside remains light and fluffy. The best grilling potatoes are the closer-textured denser potatoes, such as red, new, and boiling potatoes.

Small potatoes can be cooked whole. Rub with oil, prick the skin in a few places, and grill, covered, turning from time to time, until brown and tender, approximately 30 minutes.

Slice larger potatoes into ¾- to 1-inch slices. Rub with oil and grill until tender and brown, approximately 15 minutes per side.

Large potatoes may also be cooked whole, especially if you are grilling a roast. They require an hour or so on the grill—like an oven-baked potato. Rub with oil, prick in several places, and grill, covered, until tender when pierced with a skewer.

SQUASH

Summer is the season for both grilling and squash, and the two come together with the most delicious results. Grill zucchini whole if small, or if larger, halved lengthwise or sliced and skewered. Rub with oil and grill until tender.

Yellow or crookneck squash has a denser texture than zucchini, and is marvelous grilled. Grill whole if small; if larger halve or slice and grill on skewers until tender.

Pattypan squash is a must for the grill. Trim the top and base, and slice it in half crosswise for 2 circles of white flesh framed by pale green scalloped edges. Rub with oil and grill. Grill small pattypans whole.

TOMATOES

The sweet flavor of a fresh bright-red vine-ripened tomato goes well with any summer meal. When you find a tomato that meets these qualifications, you may hesitate to put it on the grill. But grilling helps the less-than-perfect grocery store variety.

Slice large beefsteak tomatoes into rounds and grill until hot through. Skewer cherry toma-

Vegetables for the grill

toes, and slice or quarter larger red or golden tomatoes. Plum or pear tomatoes can be halved and grilled, and green, unripe tomatoes, as well as *tomatillos,* are delicious cut into thick slices and grilled. A hinged grill may come in handy for grilling tomato slices.

TURNIPS

The much-maligned turnip, given the chance, can be a startling grill discovery. Its almost spicy potato flavor is an excellent companion for lamb, pork, duck, or game birds. The freshest turnips have the green tops attached. Buy small smooth-skinned turnips free of cracks or dried-out spots.

Slice larger turnips into ¾-inch rounds, rub with oil, and grill until browned and tender when poked with a skewer, approximately 10 to 15 minutes per side on a covered grill. Cook whole turnips, preferably small ones, on a covered grill. Rub with oil, prick several times, and bake 45 minutes or so, until tender.

YAMS AND SWEET POTATOES

These two vegetables are often confused but are easy to distinguish. The maroon or purplish yam is larger and sweeter than the light orange-skinned sweet potato. We think both are more flavorful grilled than cooked any other way. Avoid dried-out or soft yams and sweet potatoes. Select those with smooth skin and no dark spots. Slice lengthwise into ½- to ¾-inch oval slices. Rub with oil and grill, covered, until glossy brown and tender, approximately 10 to 15 minutes per side. Smaller yams or sweet potatoes can be grilled whole. Rub with oil, prick several times, and cook on a covered grill for 1 hour or more, until tender when pierced with a skewer.

A SWEET SLICE of fruit, lightly grilled, is perfect alongside many grilled foods. Grilled lamb chops are delicious with grilled pear. Chicken combines well with grilled apple slices, as does pork with pineapple. A little fruit grilled over the last glow of the fire is also a wonderful dessert. Fruit cooks best over a medium-hot to slow fire, or over a cooler part of the grill.

APPLES

The best grilling apples are slightly tart, firm, juicy apples such as Granny Smith, pippin, Gravenstein, McIntosh, Cortland, or greening. Core and halve apples, but do not peel. Rub with a little oil or butter, or marinate briefly in a little oil and white wine vinegar sweetened with honey. Grill whole halves, quarters, or slices until tender and browning, but not mushy.

BANANAS

Grilled bananas are delicious sprinkled with brown sugar and served with a dollop of ice cream or *crème fraîche*. Select firm, slightly underripe (but not green) bananas. Brush with melted butter, sweetened with a few drops of honey if desired. Grill until tender and browning, but do not allow them to become mushy. Turn bananas only once, and carefully, while grilling.

CHERRIES

Hot grilled cherries served over ice cream create a sensational dessert. If you own a cherry pitter (available in most kitchen supply stores), stem, pit, and skewer washed cherries. If not, simply stem and skewer them as close to the pit as possible. Grill until slightly soft and juicy, but not falling apart.

PEARS

The best pear varieties for the grill are the firmer fine-textured pears such as the Bartlett, Anjou, and Bosc. The Comice is a bit too fragile. Select firm pears with smooth skin and no soft spots. Halve and core, but do not peel. Rub with a little oil or butter, or marinate briefly in olive oil and white wine vinegar with a drop or two of honey. Grill until tender but *not* mushy.

PINEAPPLES

This tropical fruit is delicious sliced and grilled until lightly caramelized. Select a ripe pineapple, slightly soft to the touch and with a fragrant smell. Cut off the top, slice off the tough skin, and slice into 1-inch rounds. Grill until warm and browned. Serve alongside grilled chicken or pork, or as dessert.

STRAWBERRIES

When warmed on the grill, strawberries become soft and sweet and taste like a very fresh strawberry sauce. Wash whole large strawberries. Grill, turning a few times, until slightly soft. Serve strawberries over ice cream for a delightful dessert.

NUTS

All kinds of nuts can be roasted on the grill to sprinkle on salads, pasta, or vegetables. Try roasting raw pine nuts, walnuts, pecans, almonds, pistachios, or cashews. Coat nuts with oil and place them in a leakproof foil packet (using a square of foil). Place the packet on the coolest area of the grill. Cook the nuts, shaking the packet once or twice, for 3 to 5 minutes. It takes a little practice to cook the nuts just right, so don't be discouraged if they burn the first time.

5 | AT THE GRILL

BUTTERFLIED LEG OF LAMB WITH ZINFANDEL SAUCE

GRILLED TURNIPS
BRAISED SPINACH with TOASTED ALMONDS
CRUSTY ITALIAN BREAD
DRY RED WINE (Zinfandel)

(Serves 4)

Almost nothing compares with the flavor of grilled lamb. The sweet tender meat, which should be cooked until pink and juicy, goes perfectly with the charcoal flavor. Add dampened oak wood chips or grapevine cuttings to the coals while the lamb is cooking for flavorful smoke.

Butterflied Leg of Lamb with Zinfandel Sauce

1 leg of lamb, butterflied
Zinfandel Sauce (see page 34)

To prepare the lamb: Have your butcher remove the leg bone and "butterfly" the meat (spread it out flat). Marinate it overnight in Zinfandel Sauce. *To grill:* On a covered grill over medium-hot coals, grill the lamb 15 to 20 minutes per side. The uneven thickness of the lamb provides all degrees of doneness. To check the meat, make a small cut into the thickest part. Allow the meat to stand 15 minutes before carving. Slice ¼-inch crossgrain pieces, and serve with the Zinfandel Sauce spooned over the slices.

Grilled Turnips

Look for the smallest turnips to grill whole or halved.

12 small or 4 medium-sized turnips
Olive oil

To prepare the turnips: Scrub the turnips, do not peel. Trim the root ends. Leave whole if small. Slice larger turnips into ½-inch rounds. Rub whole turnips or slices with oil. *To grill:* On a covered grill over a medium-hot fire, cook whole small turnips for 30 minutes, or until tender when pierced with a skewer. Grill turnip halves and slices 10 to 15 minutes per side, or until tender.

Braised Spinach with Toasted Almonds

2 pounds spinach
2 tablespoons butter
Dash of salt
Freshly ground pepper
¼ cup almond slivers (see directions
for toasting nuts, page 63)

Wash the spinach leaves in several changes of cold water; stem. Drop the leaves into a pot of boiling water for 2 to 3 minutes. Drain and gently press out the excess moisture. In the same pot, melt the butter, toss in the spinach, and briefly sauté. Add salt and pepper to taste. Sprinkle toasted almond slivers on top.

VEAL CHOPS WITH GRUYÈRE AND PROSCIUTTO

GRILLED POLENTA with PESTO
GRILLED PATTYPAN SQUASH
ROASTED RED PEPPER SALAD
DRY RED WINE (Pinot Noir)

(Serves 4)

Our hearty Italian menu for *la griglia* includes tender veal chops stuffed with slices of Gruyère and prosciutto. Polenta slices are warmed on the grill, where they acquire beautiful grill marks, and are served with a dollop of *pesto*. Grill small pattypans whole. Roast the red peppers while the grill is still too hot to start the veal.

Veal Chops with Gruyère and Prosciutto

Four 1-inch-thick veal chops
4 thin slices Gruyère
4 slices prosciutto
Olive oil
1 fresh rosemary sprig
1 tablespoon chopped fresh rosemary

To prepare the chops: Make a 2-inch-deep cut along the side of each chop, forming a pocket. Inside each pocket place 1 slice each of Gruyère and prosciutto. Secure the edges with toothpicks. Brush the chops with oil using the rosemary sprigs, and sprinkle the chopped

rosemary on top. *To grill:* On an open grill over medium-hot coals, grill the chops approximately 6 minutes per side. Throw extra sprigs of rosemary on the fire as the chops grill, if desired. Remove the toothpicks and serve.

Grilled Polenta with Pesto

Polenta is a thick Italian corn cake made from coarse cornmeal (also called polenta). You can buy the cornmeal packaged as polenta, or simply labeled "coarse cornmeal." Polenta should be cooled an hour or so before cutting, and can be made a day ahead if desired.

1 teaspoon salt
4 cups water
1 cup polenta
2 tablespoons butter
Olive oil
Pesto (see page 39)

To prepare the polenta: Bring salted water to a boil in a large, heavy saucepan. Slowly add the polenta, stirring constantly with a wooden spoon. Reduce the heat and continue stirring, pressing the lumps out against the side of the pan. Cook over low heat for 45 minutes, stirring frequently, until it is thick and well congealed and pulls away from the sides of the pan. Beat in the butter. Spread the polenta into a buttered 8-inch-square pan or a 10-inch pie pan. Cool for an hour or more. Cut into squares, wedges, or strips. *To grill:* Brush the slices with olive oil. On an open grill over medium-hot coals, grill the polenta 10 minutes per side. Serve with a dollop of *pesto*.

Grilled Pattypan Squash

5 or 6 medium-sized pattypans
Olive oil

To prepare the squash: Wash the pattypans and trim the ends. Slice into ½-inch rounds and rub with oil. *To grill:* On an open grill over a medium-hot fire, grill the squash 6 minutes per side, until tender when pierced with a skewer.

Roasted Red Pepper Salad

4 red bell peppers
⅓ cup virgin olive oil
Freshly ground black pepper

To roast the peppers: Place whole peppers on an open grill over a red-hot fire. Char all sides evenly. Place the completely charred peppers in a closed paper bag for 15 minutes. Peel away the charred skin, or scrape it off with a dull knife. Remove the tops and seeds. Slice into narrow strips and marinate in the olive oil and pepper for at least 30 minutes. Serve at room temperature on a bed of Italian parsley or a leaf of red lettuce.

SKEWERED SCALLOPS, ZUCCHINI, AND ARTICHOKE HEARTS WITH SALSA

HERBED RICE
COLD LEMON ASPARAGUS
DRY WHITE WINE (Chardonnay)

(Serves 4)

Sweet and spicy flavors combine in this eclectic menu. We use large sea scallops on skewers with artichokes and zucchini. The tender sweet meat of the scallops goes well with tangy salsa, (page 39). Avoid scallops that have been frozen, as they tend to be rubbery.

Skewered Scallops, Zucchini, and Artichoke Hearts with Salsa

2½ to 3 dozen sea scallops
4 medium-sized zucchini
6 large artichoke hearts, cut into quarters, page 58,
  or 3 small jars of artichoke hearts
¼ cup olive oil
½ lime

To prepare the skewers: Soak 8 wood skewers in water for 15 minutes or so. If you are using canned artichoke hearts, drain them and reserve the oil. Wash the zucchini, trim the ends, and slice the zucchini into ½-inch rounds. Alternate the zucchini, scallops, and artichokes on the skewers, ending with approximately 4 scallops, 3 artichoke hearts, and 5 zucchini rounds per skewer (skewer and grill the extras too, of course). Brush with oil (you can use the artichoke oil if desired) and squeeze a little lime juice over the skewers. *To grill:* On an open grill over medium-hot to red-hot coals, grill the skewers, turning carefully to grill all sides evenly for a total of 6 to 8 minutes, or until the scallops are opaque. One or two skewers make one serving.

Herbed Rice

3 cups water
½ teaspoon salt
1½ cups long-grain white rice (unconverted)
1 scallion, minced, including green tops
5 cilantro sprigs, minced
½ teaspoon ground cumin
Dash of chili powder

In a large saucepan, bring the water and salt to a boil. Stir in the rice, boil again, and reduce the heat to low. Simmer, covered, for 10 minutes. Stir in the scallion, cilantro, cumin, and chili powder. Cover and continue simmering another 10 to 15 minutes, until all the water is absorbed and the rice is light and fluffy.

Cold Lemon Asparagus

Thin young asparagus is the most tender; if it is unavailable, buy the more mature asparagus and, with a vegetable peeler, peel the stalk from about 2 inches from the tip to the base.

12 to 16 asparagus spears, preferably thin stalks
⅓ cup olive oil
Juice of 1 whole lemon
½ teaspoon Dijon mustard
½ teaspoon honey
Salt and freshly ground white pepper

Wash, peel (if desired), and trim off the woody bases of the asparagus. Tie the asparagus into a bundle and steam it upright in 1½ inches of water. Cook 5 to 8 minutes, or until bright green and crunchy but not limp. Rinse under cold water and drain. Whisk the oil, lemon juice, mustard, and honey in a bowl until emulsified. Add salt and pepper to taste. Drizzle over the cold asparagus spears just before serving.

GRILLED WHOLE TROUT

GRILLED MIXED VEGETABLES with AÏOLI
ARUGULA, LIMESTONE, and RED LEAF
*   LETTUCE SALAD with AVOCADO*
DRY WHITE WINE (Chenin Blanc or Riesling)

(Serves 4)

Trout is most at home on the grill. Its delicate mild-flavored flesh absorbs flavorful smoke, and the skin becomes nicely charcoaled. Trout fresh from the stream is superior in flavor to the domestically raised rainbow variety, but any fresh trout is a treat.

Grilled Whole Trout

Avoid trout that has been frozen, as it will be bland. If possible, buy boned trout. If your trout is unboned, remove the bones after the fish is cooked, or eat around them.

> *4 fresh trout, cleaned, with head and tail still on*
> *Olive oil*
> *2 lemons, thinly sliced*
> *4 fresh basil sprigs*

To prepare the fish: Lightly brush the fish inside and out with olive oil. Place several lemon slices and 1 sprig of basil in each fish. *To grill:* On an open grill over red-hot to medium-hot coals, cook the fish approximately 5 minutes per side, until the pinkish flesh turns nearly white. Turn the fish carefully while grilling to avoid damaging the skin.

Grilled Mixed Vegetables with Aïoli

Any fresh vegetables can be used in this recipe. Select tiny ones to grill whole on skewers, or slice larger vegetables into bite-sized pieces.

> *12 tiny pattypan squash*
> *12 cherry tomatoes or 12 radishes*
> *12 mushrooms*
> *12 Brussels sprouts*
> *2 green peppers, cut into bite-sized chunks*
> *Aïoli (see page 39)*

To prepare the vegetables: Wash the vegetables but do not peel. Rub with oil. Soak 16 to 18 wood skewers in water for 15 minutes. Skewer vegetables as desired. *To grill:* On an open grill over medium-hot coals, grill the vegetables, keeping them perpendicular to the rungs of the cooking rack, until tender when pierced with a skewer. Serve with Aïoli as a dipping sauce.

Arugula, Limestone, and Red Leaf Lettuce Salad with Avocado

Arugula is a peppery-tasting green known also as rocket. If *arugula* is unavailable, use watercress. Limestone, also called Bibb lettuce, is a tender, mild lettuce; butter or Boston lettuce can be used in its place.

> *1 bunch arugula*
> *1 head limestone lettuce*
> *½ head red leaf lettuce*

> **Vinaigrette**
> *4 tablespoons virgin olive oil*
> *1½ tablespoons white wine vinegar*
> *Small pinch of sugar*
> *Dash of salt*
> *Freshly ground white pepper*
> *1 ripe avocado, cut into slices*

Wash and thoroughly dry all the greens. Mix the vinaigrette ingredients together until emulsified. Toss with the salad just before serving and garnish with avocado slices.

GRILLED STEAK WITH FRESH HERBS

GRILLED SWEET CORN
CAESAR SALAD
SOURDOUGH BREAD
DRY RED WINE (Merlot or Cabernet Sauvignon)

(Serves 4)

This classic steak menu is one of our favorites. Look for New York strip, T-bone, and porterhouse steaks, which are generally quite tender. The steaks should have plenty of marbling throughout the bright-red meat to keep it internally basted while it grills. Brush the steaks with a little oil, however, to keep them from sticking (see page 42 for more information about steaks).

Grilled Steak with Fresh Herbs

5 fresh rosemary sprigs (or basil, marjoram, sage,
*   or tarragon)*
¼ cup olive oil
Four 1½-inch-thick steaks,
*   approximately ½ to ¾ pound each*

To prepare the steaks: Using 1 or 2 herb sprigs, brush a thin layer of olive oil on each steak. Crumble a little of the herb on top. *To grill:* On an open grill over medium-hot coals, grill the steaks approximately 5 minutes per side for medium-rare (see chart on page 42 for additional cooking times). Toss the sprigs of fresh herbs on the coals as the steaks grill for an aromatic burst of smoke.

Grilled Sweet Corn

Select whole ears with the long husks still attached and not lopped off at the top.

4 ears fresh corn

To prepare the corn: Gently pull away the husk, carefully working your way down each ear to about 2 inches from the base. Avoid breaking off the husks. Pull off as much of the silk as possible. Pull the husks back up over the ear and tie at the top with a thin strip of husk. Soak in water for 15 minutes. *To grill:* Shake off the excess water and grill corn on an open or covered grill over medium-hot coals, turning several times, for 15 minutes.

Caesar Salad

The anchovies in our Caesar salad are blended into the dressing, which distinctly flavors the salad without being overly assertive.

Croutons
6 thick slices slightly stale French bread
2 tablespoons butter
2 tablespoons olive oil
1 garlic clove

2 small or 1 large head of romaine lettuce

Dressing
2 anchovy fillets
2 or 3 garlic cloves
¼ teaspoon salt
¼ cup olive oil
Juice of ½ lemon
1 teaspoon Dijon mustard
2 dashes Worcestershire sauce
1 egg yolk
3 tablespoons freshly grated Parmesan cheese

Freshly ground pepper
2 tablespoons freshly grated Parmesan cheese

To prepare the croutons: Cut the bread into ¾-inch cubes. Place on a baking sheet in 1 layer and crisp in the oven at 250° for 15 minutes. Heat the butter and olive oil in a skillet. Slightly crush the clove of garlic and sauté it over low heat for 5 minutes or so. Remove and discard. Increase the heat and sauté the dried bread cubes until brown and crisp. Drain on paper towels. *To prepare the lettuce:* Wash and thoroughly dry the leaves. Tear each leaf horizontally across the spine every 3 inches or so. *To prepare the dressing:* Mince the anchovies, garlic, and salt together on a cutting board until they form a paste. Place the paste in the bottom of a wooden salad bowl. Add the olive oil, lemon juice, mustard, Worcestershire sauce, egg yolk, and 3 tablespoons of cheese and whisk until well blended and smooth. Place the thoroughly dried lettuce in the bowl and toss. Season generously with pepper, garnish with croutons, and sprinkle the 2 tablespoons Parmesan cheese on top.

SALMON STEAKS WITH CHIVE BUTTER

GRILLED JAPANESE EGGPLANT
GRILLED SCALLIONS
COLD PASTA SALAD
DRY WHITE WINE (Sauvignon Blanc, Pinot Blanc)

(Serves 4)

Grilled salmon has a delicate texture and an exquisite flavor. Salmon was once quite abundant in our rivers and streams, and was fished like trout and cooked right over the campfire. Overfishing and pollution have promoted salmon to luxury status, but it is still at home on the backyard grill over glowing red coals.

Salmon Steaks with Chive Butter

Four 1-inch-thick salmon steaks
Olive oil
Chive Butter (see page 39)

To prepare the salmon: Brush the steaks with a little olive oil. *To grill:* On an open grill over medium-hot to red-hot coals, grill the salmon 5 to 6 minutes per side. Place a pat of Chive Butter on each hot steak and serve.

Grilled Scallions

It takes a little practice to be able to confidently maneuver long unruly scallions on the grill. Arm yourself with long-handled tongs and remember to keep the scallions *perpendicular* to the grill rungs.

10 to 12 medium-sized whole scallions
2 tablespoons olive oil
2 tablespoons white wine vinegar

To prepare the scallions: Trim 2 inches off the green tops and cut off any wilted green stalks. Trim the bases. Wash the scallions and pat dry. Marinate in the oil and vinegar for 15 to 30 minutes. *To grill:* On an open grill over medium-hot coals, grill the scallions, turning frequently, until browning and tender, approximately 10 minutes. Serve whole.

Grilled Japanese Eggplant

This narrow dark-purple eggplant is almost sweet, and its light-colored flesh becomes nicely striped on the grill. If Japanese eggplant is unavailable, slice a larger eggplant into rounds.

4 Japanese eggplants, or 1 medium-sized eggplant
Olive oil

To prepare the eggplant: Wash the eggplants but do not peel. Trim the ends, if desired, and slice each eggplant in half lengthwise. Rub with oil. *To grill:* On an open grill over medium-hot coals, grill the eggplants skin-side down for 10 minutes. Turn and grill 10 minutes more.

Cold Pasta Salad

Olive paste gives this pasta salad its unusual flavor; it is made of crushed black olives in oil and comes primarily from France and Italy. Olive paste is sold in jars; you can find it, as well as dried tomatoes packed in oil, in Italian markets. Use roasted red peppers if the tomatoes are unavailable.

1 tablespoon salt
1 tablespoon oil
1 pound dried fusilli (spiral pasta)

Sauce
¼ cup olive oil
3 tablespoons olive paste
2 teaspoons rice vinegar or distilled white vinegar
1 tablespoon heavy cream
6 to 7 whole sun-dried tomatoes, drained on paper towels and sliced into long, thin strips

To prepare the pasta: Add the salt and oil to a large pot of water and bring to a boil. Pour in the pasta and cook until tender, 8 to 10 minutes. Drain and cool. *To prepare the sauce:* Combine the oil, olive paste, vinegar, and cream in a bowl. Whisk to emulsify. Add the tomatoes. Pour over the pasta and toss, coating all the pieces evenly.

TOFU MARINATED IN SESAME OIL AND RICE VINEGAR WITH SCALLIONS

GRILLED WHOLE CHILIES
SLICED FRESH FRUIT
COLD SOBA NOODLES
SPARKLING WATER with LEMON ZEST

(Serves 4)

Tofu, one of the world's "future foods," is high in protein and low in carbohydrates and cholesterol. Because of its very mild taste, it offers the distinct advantage of picking up nearly any flavor it is cooked with, making it quite versatile. Our sesame oil and rice vinegar marinade combines with grill smoke to uniquely flavor the tofu in this menu. Add dampened wood chips or aromatic herbs to the coals for more smoke.

Tofu Marinated in Sesame Oil and Rice Vinegar with Scallions

Buy tofu labeled "firm" in the vegetable or refrigerated cheese section of most grocery stores. Drain off the liquid and place tofu between several layers of paper towels with a weight on top. Drain 1 to 3 hours.

> *Two 1-pound packages "firm" tofu, drained*
> *2 tablespoons dark sesame oil (see page 34)*
> *3 tablespoons rice vinegar or distilled white vinegar*
> *4 tablespoons tamari (page 34), or soy sauce*

To prepare the tofu: Cut the drained tofu into four ¾-inch slices. Mix the sesame oil, rice vinegar, and *tamari*. Marinate the tofu, turning frequently, for 1 hour. Soak 2 wood skewers in water for 15 minutes or so. With the tofu pieces lying flat, insert the skewers parallel to each other horizontally into the tofu. To grill: Place the tofu on an open grill over a medium-hot fire. Cook 5 minutes, turn, and cook another 8 minutes, until the outside is slightly crispy and brown.

Grilled Whole Chilies

Select fresh mild chilies, such as the long green *poblano*, *ancho*, or *Anaheim*.

> *4 whole green chilies*

To grill chilies: On an open grill over medium-hot coals, grill the chilies, turning frequently, until light brown and tender. Slice along the side of the chili and remove the seeds. Serve whole or remove the tops, as desired.

Sliced Fresh Fruit

This tart and refreshing fruit dish can be served as a salad or dessert. Select firm ripe fruit in season, such as peaches, honeydew, kiwi, green grapes, green apples, cantaloupe, pears, and plums.

> *Fruit*
> *½ cup plain yogurt*
> *1 teaspoon honey*
> *Chopped fresh mint*
> *Mint sprigs*

Slice the fruit. Serve with a dollop of yogurt mixed with honey and mint. Garnish with mint sprigs.

Cold Soba Noodles

Soba noodles are quite popular in Japan, and are just starting to catch on in this country. Made from buckwheat, they are high in protein and have a nice flavor and texture. They are sold dried and packaged in Asian markets or the specialty section of some grocery stores.

> *½ pound soba noodles*
> *2 tablespoons peanut or safflower oil*
> *3 tablespoons rice vinegar or distilled white vinegar*
> *2 teaspoons tamari (page 34) or soy sauce*
> *1 teaspoon dark sesame oil (page 34)*
> *1½ teaspoons minced fresh ginger*
> *1 tablespoon coarsely chopped fresh cilantro*
> *1 carrot, cut into small 1-inch sticks*
> *Sesame seeds*

Place the noodles in a large pot of boiling salted water and boil 5 to 7 minutes, until tender. Drain and rinse under cool water. Set aside to drain. Mix the oil, vinegar, *tamari*, sesame oil, ginger, and cilantro together in a bowl. Add the noodles and carrot and toss well. Garnish each serving with sesame seeds.

ROCK CORNISH GAME HENS IN RASPBERRY VINEGAR MARINADE

GRILLED PEARS
GRILLED MUSHROOMS
STEAMED FRESH GREEN BEANS
  with WATER CHESTNUTS
DRY WHITE WINE (Chardonnay)

(Serves 4)

Rock Cornish game hens are all-white-meat birds. Though they are raised on farms, they have a slightly gamey taste that combines well with the fruit marinade and grilled pears in this menu. Hens are grilled split in this recipe, but they can be grilled whole or butterflied as well. We estimate one-half hen per serving, but you may want to cook an extra one.

Rock Cornish Game Hens in Raspberry Vinegar Marinade

Though many grocery stores sell frozen hens, fresh ones are becoming more common and are worth looking for.

> *2 Rock Cornish game hens*
> *Raspberry Vinegar Marinade (see page 34)*

To prepare the hens: Rinse whole hens and pat dry. Split in half lengthwise, cutting all the way through with a heavy sharp knife. Marinate 1 to 3 hours. *To grill:* On an open grill over medium-hot coals, sear the skin side 1 to 2 minutes, turn, and sear the other side. Cover and cook 25 minutes, turning and basting twice during grilling.

Grilled Pears

Select firm, slightly underripe pears for the grill.

> *2 medium-sized pears*
> *1 tablespoon walnut oil or olive oil*
> *2 tablespoons rice vinegar or distilled white vinegar*
> *½ teaspoon honey*

To prepare the pears: Wash, stem, slice in half lengthwise, and core. Do not peel. Marinate the pears in oil, vinegar, and honey for 15 to 30 minutes. *To grill:* On an open or covered grill over a medium-hot fire, grill the pears skin-side down for 10 minutes. Turn and grill another 5 minutes, or until tender when pierced with a skewer.

Grilled Mushrooms

> *16 to 20 medium-sized mushrooms*
> *Raspberry Vinegar Marinade, above, or oil*

To prepare the mushrooms: Wash and trim the stems. Marinate the mushrooms in some of the Raspberry Vinegar Marinade for 15 minutes, or brush with oil. Soak 4 wood skewers in water for 15 minutes or so. Place 4 or 5 mushrooms on each skewer. *To grill:* On an open or covered grill over medium-hot coals, grill the mushrooms 15 minutes, turning frequently to brown all sides.

Steamed Fresh Green Beans with Water Chestnuts

> *1 pound fresh green beans*
> *2 tablespoons butter*
> *¼ cup sliced canned water chestnuts*
> *Salt and freshly ground pepper*

Wash and trim the beans. Steam until bright green but still crunchy, approximately 8 minutes. Melt the butter in a skillet, add the beans and water chestnuts, and sauté 3 minutes or so. Season to taste.

SESAME FLANK STEAK

GRILLED WHOLE POTATOES
SAUTÉED FRESH OKRA
SLICED TOMATOES with OLIVE OIL and BASIL
DRY RED WINE (Pinot Noir or Gamay Beaujolais)

(Serves 4)

Flank steak is a delicious alternative to expensive steak cuts when cooked and carved with a little attention. Always marinate flank steak overnight to tenderize it and add flavor, and cook it quickly over a red-hot fire. The seared in juices leave a flavorful pink interior. Carve the flat steak at a deep angle for oval slices.

Flank Steak with Sesame Marinade

We love cold grilled flank steak on sandwiches the next day, so we always grill 2 steaks with this plentiful marinade.

> *Flank steak, approximately 1½ pounds*
> *Sesame Marinade (see page 34)*

To prepare the steak: Marinate the steak overnight, turning 2 or 3 times. *To grill:* On an open grill over a red-hot to medium-hot fire, first sear the flank steak 1 minute per side. Continue cooking 5 to 6 minutes per side, turning once. *To carve:* Place the steak flat on a carving board. With a sharp knife positioned almost flat to the top of the steak, cut thin slices diagonally across the grain, for wide oval pieces. Spoon the juices over the slices.

Grilled Whole Potatoes

> *8 small potatoes*
> *Olive oil*

To prepare the potatoes: Scrub the potatoes but do not peel. Rub each potato with olive oil. *To grill:* On a covered grill over medium-hot coals, grill the potatoes until tender when pierced with a skewer, approximately 30 minutes. Turn frequently while grilling to brown all sides.

Sautéed Fresh Okra

Okra is an unusual summer vegetable with a mild flavor and a crunchy texture.

> *1 pound fresh okra*
> *4 tablespoons butter*
> *2 shallots, chopped*
> *Salt and freshly ground pepper*

Wash the okra and trim the stems, if desired. Drop into a pot of boiling water and blanch for 1 minute. Drain. In a large skillet, melt the butter over medium-high heat and sauté the okra and shallots for 3 to 4 minutes, tossing to coat the okra evenly. Season to taste and serve.

Sliced Tomatoes with Olive Oil and Basil

> *3 to 4 large red-ripe tomatoes*
> *2 tablespoons tiny basil leaves*
> *⅓ cup virgin olive oil*
> *Salt and freshly ground black pepper*

Wash the tomatoes and basil. Slice the tomatoes ¼ inch thick and arrange on a platter. Sprinkle the basil leaves over the slices. Pour the olive oil over the tomatoes and let stand at room temperature for 30 minutes. Season to taste with salt and freshly ground black pepper.

BONELESS PORK LOIN IN SHERRY VINEGAR, PORT, AND PRUNE MARINADE

GRILLED CARROTS
HERBED POTATOES
TOSSED GREENS
DRY RED WINE (Gamay Beaujolais)

(Serves 4)

The hearty flavor of port and the delicate sweetness of prunes combine in this elegant recipe for pork. The pitted prunes become infused with the wine and are intoxicatingly delicious. Arrange them over grilled pork slices.

Boneless Pork Loin in Sherry Vinegar, Port and Prune Marinade

1½ pounds boneless rolled pork loin roast, tied with string
Sherry Vinegar, Port, and Prune Marinade (see page 35)

To prepare the pork: Marinate the pork roast for 3 hours. *To grill:* On an open grill over medium-hot coals, sear all sides of the roast for 10 minutes, turning

frequently. Cover and cook 20 to 30 minutes, or until a meat thermometer reaches 110°. Remove and slice into 1-inch slices. Brush the slices liberally with marinade and return to the grill. Grill another 4 to 5 minutes per side with the cover off.

Grilled Carrots

1 dozen small carrots
Olive oil

To prepare the carrots: Wash but do not peel the carrots. Trim the tops, if desired, and rub the carrots with olive oil. *To grill:* On an open or closed grill over medium-hot coals, cook carrots 10 to 15 minutes, turning frequently, until browning and tender when pierced with a skewer.

Herbed Potatoes

4 medium-sized baking potatoes
2 tablespoons butter
¼ cup half and half
3 ounces Gruyère, grated (1½ cups)
3 tablespoons coarsely chopped fresh chives
Dash of nutmeg
Salt and pepper to taste

Scrub the potatoes but do not peel them. Quarter. In a large pot of boiling water, boil the potatoes for 10 to 15 minutes, or until tender when pierced with a skewer. Drain and coarsely mash the potatoes with the butter, half and half, 1¼ cups of the cheese, chives, and nutmeg. Season to taste. Spread the potatoes evenly in a buttered 8-by-10-inch or oval baking dish. Sprinkle the remaining cheese on top and heat for 15 minutes in a preheated 350° oven. Brown the top under a broiler and serve.

Tossed Greens

1 head butter or Boston lettuce
½ head escarole

Dressing
½ cup plain yogurt
1 tablespoon olive oil
1 tablespoon white wine vinegar
1 tablespoon minced fresh parsley
1 tablespoon minced fresh chives
Small pinch of sugar
Salt and pepper to taste
½ cucumber, sliced into rounds

Wash and thoroughly dry the greens and mix them together in a salad bowl. Combine the dressing ingredients in a bowl and whisk until smooth. Toss the salad just before serving and arrange cucumber slices over the top of each serving.

GRILLED SPLIT LOBSTER TAIL

ROASTED GARLIC HEADS
BUTTER LETTUCE and WATERCRESS SALAD
BAGUETTE
DRY WHITE WINE (Chardonnay)

(Serves 4)

Shellfish is at its best on the grill, and lobster is no exception. Its juicy white meat cooks quickly, absorbing flavorful grill smoke. If cooked just until it has barely turned opaque, lobster will be succulent and tender. Alongside the sweet lobster are whole heads of garlic, coated with olive oil and roasted over the coals. Each clove is reduced to a mild, savory paste to squeeze onto slices of crusty baguette. Start the grill about 1¼ hours before you plan to eat, allowing 45 minutes for the coals to light and 30 minutes for the garlic to cook. The garlic should be done when you start the lobster. Remove the hood for the last 10 minutes of the garlic cooking time to fire up the coals for the lobster.

Grilled Split Lobster Tail

4 medium-sized lobster tails
White Wine Butter Sauce (see page 38)

To prepare the lobster: Rinse each tail and pat dry. Place shell-side down on a cutting board. With a heavy knife, cut in half lengthwise down the middle, slicing right through the shell. Marinate ½ hour in the butter sauce. *To grill:* On an open grill over a medium- to red-hot fire, place the tails flesh-side down. Cook 5 minutes. Turn flesh-side up and baste. Cook another 3 to 5 minutes, or until the flesh is opaque and the shells bright red. Two halves make 1 serving. Serve the sauce for dipping, if desired.

Roasted Garlic Heads

2 plump whole heads of garlic
½ cup olive oil
2 teaspoons minced fresh thyme or rosemary,
   or 1 teaspoon dried
Dash of salt
Freshly ground pepper

To prepare the garlic: Peel away some of the papery outer layers, particularly from down among the top cloves on the head. Do not pierce or expose the cloves. Form sheets of heavy aluminum foil into 2 small cup shapes, or use a small pie tin for each head. Place the garlic in the cups and pour three-fourths of the olive oil over them, allowing it to settle in between the cloves and on the bottom of the tin. Sprinkle the herb, salt, and pepper over the top. *To grill:* On a covered grill over

a medium-hot fire, bake the garlic for 30 to 40 minutes, basting twice with the remaining oil. The garlic is done when the heads are brown and the cloves seem empty or mushy when poked. *To serve:* Place the garlic heads on a plate and pour the oil over them. Peel off a clove and squeeze the paste out of the bottom onto the bread. Soak up some oil with the bread before squeezing on the garlic, if desired.

Butter Lettuce and Watercress Salad

1 medium-sized head of butter or Boston lettuce
½ bunch watercress

Vinaigrette
4 tablespoons walnut oil or olive oil
1 tablespoon red wine vinegar
Dash of sugar
Dash of salt
Freshly ground pepper to taste

¼ cup Niçoise olives
1 tablespoon grated orange zest

Wash and dry the greens thoroughly. Combine all the vinaigrette ingredients in a bowl and whisk until emulsified. Toss with the greens, olives, and orange zest just before serving.

Mixed Sausage Grill

GRILLED RED ONION QUARTERS
RED CABBAGE with APPLES
DARK GERMAN BREAD
GERMAN or DUTCH BEER

(Serves 4)

Sausages seem destined to be the wave of the future (or, perhaps more accurately, a revival of the past). More interesting varieties are becoming available, and more delicatessens, butchers, and ethnic markets are starting to make and sell their own. Sausages are inexpensive and are delicious when freshly made without preservatives or too much salt.

Sausages are at their best grilled, because the skin crisps and browns while excess fat drips off. Serve them with several types of mustard, dense rich German brown or rye bread, and sweet and dill pickles.

Mixed Sausage Grill

Try all types of sausages on the grill, such as mild or hot Italian sausages, *bockwurst,* French wine sausages, garlic sausages, bratwurst, *linguiça,* knockwurst, and kielbasa.

10 to 12 sausages of different varieties

To prepare the sausages: Separate any linked sausages. Prick the skins in a few places with a skewer. *To grill:* Cook sausages on a covered grill over a medium-hot fire. Sausages may cause flare-ups, so be prepared to move them to cooler spots on the grill with long-handled tongs. Turn sausages frequently as they grill, to brown all sides. Sausages require 15 to 20 minutes on the grill, depending on size and content. To test, cut into one and if still pink, continue grilling.

Grilled Red Onion Quarters

Sweet red onions lightly caramelize on the grill, becoming slightly soft and mild.

2 medium-sized sweet red or white onions
Olive oil

To prepare the onions: Trim both ends of the onions and peel. Cut into quarters. Soak 16 short wood skewers in water for 15 or so minutes. Rub each quarter of onion with olive oil and skewer in 2 places through all the layers, placing 2 or 3 quarters on each skewer. *To grill:* On an open grill over medium-hot coals, grill onions until browning and tender, approximately 10 minutes per side.

Red Cabbage with Apples

This modified sauerkraut is a sweet and colorful accompaniment to the sausages and onions.

1½ pounds red cabbage (1 medium-sized head)
2 tart green apples, cored and thinly sliced
2 tablespoons butter
2 tablespoons olive oil
2 medium-sized onions, halved and thinly sliced
1 tablespoon brown sugar
½ teaspoon caraway seeds
½ teaspoon ground coriander
⅛ teaspoon grated nutmeg
Salt and freshly ground pepper to taste
¼ cup dry red wine
2 tablespoons cider vinegar

Slice the cabbage into ¼-inch-wide strips. Rinse under running water in a colander, shaking the strips into a loose bunch. Steam the cabbage for 5 minutes. Add the apples and steam another 2 to 3 minutes. Remove and run under cold water. Set aside to drain. In a large pot, melt the butter and oil. Sauté the onions, sugar, and spices until soft, approximately 10 minutes. Add the wine and vinegar and simmer a minute or so over medium-high heat. Add the cabbage and apples and toss, cooking another 2 minutes. Remove from heat and serve.

CHICKEN BREASTS IN MANY MUSTARDS

GRILLED GRAVENSTEIN APPLE SLICES
GRILLED BABY LEEKS
RADICCHIO SALAD
DRY WHITE WINE (Chardonnay)

(Serves 4)

On the grill the tart mustards blend and mellow, becoming smoky, rich, and flavorful. Sweet grilled apple slices and leeks are complementary accompaniments. *Radicchio,* an Italian chicory with beautiful brilliant-red leaves, is prized for its peppery flavor. Serve this salad at the end of the meal.

Chicken Breasts in Many Mustards

4 half breasts of chicken, boned and skinned
Mustard Marinade (see page 36)

To prepare the chicken: Marinate 2 to 4 hours. *To grill:* On an open grill over medium-hot coals, cook the chicken 6 to 7 minutes per side. Spoon the marinade over the grilled chicken as a sauce, if desired.

Grilled Gravenstein Apple Slices

McIntoshes and Gravensteins, small, firm, and slightly tart red/green apples, become slightly sweet on the grill. Other tart red or green apples, such as Granny Smith, pippin, or Cortland, are also good.

3 Gravenstein apples
Walnut oil
White wine vinegar

To prepare the apples: Wash, core, and cut the apples into ¼-inch slices. Rub with walnut oil and sprinkle with vinegar. *To grill:* On an open grill over medium-hot coals, cook the apples until tender when pierced with a skewer, approximately 3 minutes per side. Serve each grilled chicken breast over 2 or 3 apple slices.

Grilled Baby Leeks

Baby leeks are the sweetest and have the best texture, and are a bit easier to manage on the grill. Avoid dried-out looking leeks or those with withered bases.

¼ cup olive oil
¼ cup white wine vinegar
6 or 7 thin slices of orange zest
1 teaspoon chopped fresh thyme, or a pinch of dried
Freshly ground white pepper
12 baby or 2 large leeks

To prepare the leeks: Combine the oil, vinegar, orange zest, thyme, and pepper in a bowl and let stand while you prepare the leeks. To remove the grit from small leeks, split down the middle lengthwise to 2 inches from the base. Rinse the grit out from between the layers and shake dry. Trim off about 3 inches of the green top and trim the base, if desired. Marinate 15 to 30 minutes in the oil-vinegar mixture. For larger leeks, split in half lengthwise, rinse, secure the layers with toothpicks, and marinate. *To grill:* On an open grill over medium-hot coals, grill the leeks on all sides until browning and tender, 10 to 15 minutes.

Radicchio Salad

Try curly endive, Belgian endive, or watercress if *radicchio* is unavailable.

2 heads radicchio
¼ cup whole walnuts

Vinaigrette
6 tablespoons walnut oil
2 tablespoons sherry vinegar
1 teaspoon Dijon mustard
Small pinch of sugar
Dash of salt
Freshly ground pepper

Wash the *radicchio* leaves carefully and pat dry. Combine the vinaigrette ingredients in a bowl and whisk to emulsify. Toss the salad just before serving and sprinkle walnuts on top.

NAM PRIK SHRIMP

GRILLED ZUCCHINI
TOMATO PASTA with OLIVE OIL and
   LEMON ZEST
DRY WHITE WINE (Sauvignon Blanc, Pinot Blanc)

(Serves 4)

Many shrimp or prawn varieties have vividly colored shells and exotic markings. We used tiger shrimp for this spicy recipe. They are extra large and meaty, and have a sweet, delicate flavor that combines well with the hot chili marinade. Substitute any large shrimp; select fresh ones (not frozen) with firm, translucent flesh.

Nam Prik Shrimp

Our *nam prik,* or "spicy," shrimp is made by combining green and red chili slivers in oil, vinegar, and red chili paste.

> *12 jumbo shrimp*
> *Nam Prik Marinade (see page 35)*

To prepare the shrimp: Shell, beginning at the "head": separate the shell on the underside and work your way down, pulling the shell away gently. With a paring knife, remove the vein visible just under the flesh along the back. Rinse and pat dry. Marinate in Nam Prik Marinade for ½ hour. *To skewer:* Soak 4 wood skewers in water for 15 minutes or so. Thread 3 shrimp on each skewer, piercing at the head and tail, as pictured. *To grill:* On an open grill over red-hot to medium-hot fire, grill the shrimp 2 to 3 minutes per side, basting once after the first turn. Shrimp is done when just pink and opaque. Each skewer is one serving.

Grilled Zucchini

Use whole small or medium-sized zucchini, sliced lengthwise into halves for this recipe.

> *2 small zucchini*
> *2 tablespoons olive oil*
> *2 tablespoons champagne vinegar or white wine vinegar*

To prepare the zucchini: Wash the zucchini but do not peel. Trim the ends if desired. Rub the zucchini with oil and sprinkle with vinegar. *To grill:* On an open or covered grill over a medium-hot fire, grill the zucchini for 10 to 12 minutes, turning frequently, until tender when pierced with a skewer.

Tomato Pasta with Olive Oil and Lemon Zest

Tomato pasta can be found in gourmet markets, and it is usually sold fresh. You can substitute spinach or beet pasta in this recipe.

> *1 tablespoon salt*
> *1 pound tomato pasta*
> *¼ cup virgin olive oil*
> *1 cup freshly grated Parmesan cheese*
> *Salt and freshly ground pepper to taste*
> *1 lemon*

To a large pot of water add the salt and bring to a boil. Boil fresh pasta approximately 5 minutes, or until tender; dried pasta usually takes 5 to 8 minutes. Drain. Toss with the olive oil and Parmesan cheese, and season with salt and pepper. Using a lemon zester, peel off thin strips of lemon zest. Sprinkle the lemon zest on top.

GRILLED BREAST OF DUCK IN RED WINE MARINADE

GRILLED CROOKNECK SQUASH
WILD RICE with GREEN ONIONS
  and MUSHROOMS
BELGIAN ENDIVE SALAD
  with TOASTED PINE NUTS
DRY RED WINE (Pinot Noir)

(Serves 4)

This hearty menu is perfect for one of those fall days when the weather is starting to get cool and crisp. Rich, flavorful duck is excellent grilled. To prevent flare-ups, grill duck over indirect heat with a drip pan underneath (for an explanation of indirect cooking, see page 28). Toss aromatic herbs onto the coals to add flavorful smoke, if desired.

Grilled Breast of Duck in Red Wine Marinade

2 boned duck breasts, split into halves
Red Wine Marinade (see page 34)

To prepare the duck: Pull off any chunks of fat. Prick the skin in a few places and marinate overnight. *To grill:* Prepare a medium-hot indirect fire. Sear the duck flesh-side down for 2 minutes. Turn and sear the skin side 2 minutes. Turn back to the flesh side, cover, and cook 10 minutes. Turn again, cover, and cook another 5 to 10 minutes.

Grilled Crookneck Squash

Also called summer squash, this pretty yellow vegetable is delicious on the grill.

2 medium-sized crookneck squash
Olive oil

To prepare the squash: Wash the squash and trim the ends. Slice the squash lengthwise in halves. Rub with oil. *To grill:* On an open or closed grill over medium-hot coals, grill approximately 8 minutes per side.

Wild Rice with Green Onions and Mushrooms

1 cup wild rice
4 cups water
1 teaspoon salt
2 tablespoons butter
3 scallions, chopped
6 to 8 mushrooms, halved or quartered
Salt and freshly ground pepper

In a strainer or colander, thoroughly rinse the rice under cold running water. Place in a heavy saucepan with the water and salt. Bring to a boil, stir, and simmer covered approximately 45 minutes. The kernels should be popped open and tender, but not mushy. Drain well. Melt the butter in a large skillet and sauté the scallions and mushrooms 2 to 3 minutes. Stir in the rice. Toss and season to taste.

Belgian Endive Salad with Toasted Pine Nuts

¼ cup pine nuts
Oil
3 heads Belgian endive

Vinaigrette
4 tablespoons walnut oil
1 tablespoon red wine vinegar
½ garlic clove, minced
1 teaspoon minced fresh basil, or a pinch dried
Salt and freshly ground pepper

Toast the pine nuts, coated lightly with oil, in a foil packet on the grill for 3 to 5 minutes. Carefully separate the endive heads into leaves. Wash and dry the leaves, and set 5 whole leaves aside for garnish. Slice the leaves lengthwise into thin strips. Combine all the vinaigrette ingredients in a small bowl and whisk to emulsify. Toss the salad just before serving. Garnish with whole leaves and toasted pine nuts.

PEANUT CHICKEN ON SKEWERS

RICE with LEMON GRASS and COCONUT
CARROT SALAD with GREEN PAPAYA
LAGER BEER

(Serves 4)

Peanut Chicken is our variation on *satay*, the Indonesian dish of skewered and grilled slices of beef dipped in peanut sauce. We marinate the chicken before grilling, and serve the sauce for dipping. Tangy carrot salad is served with slivers of unripened papaya. A tall cold bottle of Thai beer, or any full-bodied lager beer, is the perfect balance for this combination of spicy and sweet flavors.

Peanut Chicken on Skewers

6 half chicken breasts, boned and skinned
Peanut Marinade (see page 34)
12 scallions

To prepare the chicken: Cut the half-breasts into bite-sized chunks. Mix well in the Peanut Marinade, coating the chicken pieces evenly, and marinate for at least 2 hours. Stir the chicken 2 or 3 times as it marinates to coat all the pieces. *To prepare the skewers:* Soak 12 wood skewers in water for 15 minutes or so. Thread 5 or 6 chunks of chicken onto each skewer. Trim 3 inches of green off the tops of the scallions, and slice each in half crosswise. Skewer the halves on each end of the chicken skewers. *To grill:* On an open grill over a medium-hot fire, grill the skewered chicken for 8 to 10 minutes, turning after 2 or 3 minutes to grill all sides evenly. Two or three skewers make one serving. *Note:* The chicken skewers are easiest to turn with long-handled tongs. Avoid clamping onto the onions, as they tear easily.

Rice with Lemon Grass and Coconut

2 cups water
1½ cups long-grain white rice (unconverted)
½ cup coconut milk (see note)
2 tablespoons minced fresh lemon grass,
* or 2 teaspoons dried (see note)*
1 teaspoon unsweetened coconut flakes

Bring the water to a boil in a large covered saucepan. Stir in the rice and bring back to a boil. Stir again, cover, and reduce the heat to a slow simmer. After 10 minutes, pour in the coconut milk and add the lemon grass and coconut flakes. Simmer until all the moisture is absorbed, approximately 10 minutes more. Let the rice stand a minute or so with the lid slightly askew, and serve. Place 3 skewers of chicken per plate over a mound of rice.

Note: You can find coconut milk canned in the specialty section of most grocery stores. It will be labeled as such, and should contain nothing more than the milky white extract from the white flesh. Lemon grass is an herb that originated in India but has flourished in many East Asian cuisines, including Thai and Vietnamese. It is available fresh or dried in Asian markets.

Carrot Salad with Green Papaya

Juice of ½ lemon
Juice of 1 whole lime
1 tablespoon light soy sauce or fish sauce
1 tablespoon rice vinegar or distilled white vinegar
Small pinch of sugar
1 pound carrots, grated
½ dried red chili pepper, minced
½ cup julienned unripened papaya or cucumber
2 tablespoons minced fresh parsley
½ cup roasted peanuts, minced

Combine the lemon juice, lime juice, soy sauce, vinegar, and sugar in a bowl. Whisk to blend. To the shredded carrots add the dried pepper, green papaya, parsley, and chopped peanuts. Pour the liquid over the carrots and toss well. Serve at room temperature. Carrot salad can be prepared a half day in advance and kept in the refrigerator until 30 minutes before serving.

BARBECUED BABY BACK PORK RIBS IN HONEY, TAMARI, AND ORANGE MARINADE

GRILLED YAM SLICES
WALDORF SALAD
CORN MUFFINS with GREEN CHILIES
BEER

(Serves 4)

Nothing is more inviting than the classic smell of barbecuing ribs mingled with the sweet aroma of hickory wood smoke. We use baby back ribs, but spareribs are also delicious though not as meaty. Country-style ribs are the meatiest and are sold individually. We like to oven-bake our ribs for 40 minutes before grilling. This keeps them moist and prevents the outside from becoming overly charred on the grill. Marinate ribs up to 48 hours.

Barbecued Baby Back Pork Ribs in Honey, Tamari, and Orange Marinade

Also try Asian Barbecue Marinade, Traditional Barbecue Sauce, or New American Spicy Barbecue Sauce for ribs.

> *2 meaty baby back rib racks, or approximately 1½ pounds per person*
> *A double recipe of Honey, Tamari, and Orange Marinade (see page 35)*

To prepare the ribs: Marinate the ribs from 24 to 48 hours, turning several times. Place in a baking pan (reserving the marinade in a bowl) and bake at 350° for 40 minutes. *To grill:* Place the baked ribs on a closed grill over medium-hot coals and grill 10 to 15 minutes per side, basting frequently, until glazed brown and tender. Carve off individual ribs to serve. *Note:* Have your butcher crack the ribs along the backbone to make them easier to carve.

Grilled Yam Slices

> *2 medium-sized yams*
> *Olive oil*

To prepare the yams: Scrub the skins but do not peel. Trim the ends. Slice the yams lengthwise into ¾-inch-thick slices. Rub with oil. *To grill:* On an open or closed grill over a medium-hot fire, cook the yam slices approximately 10 minutes per side, or until tender when pierced with a skewer.

Waldorf Salad

> *1 firm ripe red apple*
> *2 firm green apples*
> *½ lemon*

> **Sauce**
> *⅓ cup mayonnaise*
> *2 tablespoons heavy cream*
> *1 teaspoon white wine vinegar*
> *Juice of ¼ lemon*
> *1 teaspoon honey*
> *1 teaspoon minced fresh ginger*
> *Dash of salt*
> *Freshly ground pepper to taste*

> *½ cup coarsely chopped walnuts*
> *2 celery stalks, sliced into ¼-inch pieces*
> *¼ cup raisins*
> *2 scallions, minced*

Wash, core, quarter, and thinly slice the apples. Squeeze a little lemon juice over them to keep them from darkening. Whisk the sauce ingredients together in a small bowl. Add the nuts, celery, raisins, and scallions to the apples and toss. Pour the sauce over the apples and mix well to coat all pieces evenly.

Corn Muffins with Green Chilies

This recipe makes 12 muffins.

> *1 cup yellow cornmeal*
> *¾ cup unbleached flour*
> *⅓ cup dark brown sugar*
> *2 teaspoons baking powder*
> *1 teaspoon baking soda*
> *¼ teaspoon salt*
> *1 large egg*
> *¾ cup milk*
> *1 tablespoon melted butter*
> *¾ cup fresh or frozen corn kernels*
> *¼ cup canned diced green chilies, drained*

Generously grease 2 muffin tins or corn muffin pans. Thoroughly combine the cornmeal, flour, brown sugar, baking powder, baking soda, and salt in a large bowl. In another bowl, beat the egg, milk, and melted butter together. Stir into the cornmeal mixture and blend well. Stir in the corn and green chilies. Spoon into muffin cups to ¾ full. Bake in a preheated 425° oven for 15 minutes, or until the tops are browned and a skewer inserted in the center comes out clean.

GRILL APPETIZER PARTY

TOPINKA
GRILLED OYSTERS and CLAMS on the SHELL
DRY SPARKLING WINE (Brut) or
DRY WHITE WINE (Sauvignon Blanc)

(Serves 8)

The hissing and popping of fresh oysters and clams on the grill and the aroma of garlic, cheese, and mesquite are too alluring to resist. Everyone will want to participate, and with several sets of hands equipped with tongs and mitts, the production line of *topinka*, oysters, and clams need never be broken.

Topinka

Topinka is a Czechoslovakian appetizer of broiled cheese and garlic on dense rye bread. Ours is adapted for the grill from some we had at Britt-Marie's restaurant in Berkeley, California.

> *½ stick (¼ cup) butter*
> *2 garlic cloves, minced*
> *Dash of freshly ground white pepper*
> *Dense dark rye bread, thinly sliced, or 3 dozen slices*
> *cocktail rye or pumpernickel bread*
> *½ pound Emmenthaler cheese, thinly sliced*
> *Paprika*

To prepare the ingredients: In a small saucepan, melt the butter and sauté the garlic for 2 to 3 minutes over low heat; add the pepper. Have the bread, garlic butter, cheese slices, and paprika near the grill. Brush both sides of the bread with butter. *To grill:* On an open grill over a medium-hot to red-hot fire, grill one side of the bread until golden brown, 2 to 3 minutes. Remove. On the grilled side, spoon a little garlic onto the bread and place a slice of cheese over the top. Grill cheese-side up until the cheese is melted and the underside of the bread is golden brown. Sprinkle with paprika and serve.

Grilled Oysters

We can't resist testing an oyster or two before they go on the grill, but purists who say an oyster should never be cooked owe it to themselves to try them on the grill.

> *3 dozen fresh oysters in the shell*
> *White Wine Butter Sauce (see page 38)*

To prepare the oysters: Fresh oysters should be tightly closed or should close up when handled. Discard any open or abnormally lightweight shells. Scrub the oyster shells under running water. Store in a bowl or paper bag in the refrigerator. *To grill:* Place the oysters on an open grill over a red-hot to medium-hot fire with the flat shell up. Cook until the shells pop open (this isn't very dramatic, so look carefully), approximately 4 to 6 minutes. Discard any that do not open. Remove the oysters with tongs, taking care not to spill the juices. Wearing a mitt, hold each oyster bowl-side up and gently pull off the top shell. If the oyster is still clinging to the top shell, gently scrape it into the bottom shell. Spoon a little White Wine Butter Sauce into each shell and place it carefully on the grill. Grill 2 to 3 more minutes, until the sauce is bubbly and browning. Use small skewers or toothpicks to eat the tender, juicy morsels.

Grilled Clams

Clams steam inside their round shells and pop wide open when they are ready. Dip them in a little sauce or salsa, or just have them straight off the grill.

> *3 dozen medium-sized clams in the shell*

To prepare the clams: Fresh clams are either tightly closed or will close when rapped. Discard any open or abnormally light shells. Scrub the shells under running water. Soak clams in several changes of salted water for 45 minutes to 1 hour to encourage them to spit out sand and grit. *To grill:* Toss the clams on an open grill over a red-hot to medium-hot fire. When done, they will pop wide open, in approximately 5 to 7 minutes. Discard any that do not open. Remove and eat, using small skewers or toothpicks to retrieve the clams.

GRILL MANUFACTURERS

Arkla

All sizes of outdoor gas grills
P.O. Box 534
Evansville, IN

Barbecues Galore

Cook-On Turbo
The "Aussie Barbie," a wagon-style gas grill with hood and rotisserie. Barbecues Galore is also a retail store, and sells many other brands of grills in its stores.

14048 East Firestone Boulevard
Santa Fe Springs, CA 90670
(714) 522-0660
(213) 921-7141

18922 Ventura Boulevard
Tarzana, CA 91356
(818) 435-7314

Broilmaster

All sizes of outdoor gas grills
LSC Incorporated
P.O. Box 1760
Kansas City, MO 64141

Charbroil

All sizes of charcoal and gas grills, smokers, accessories
W.C. Bradley Enterprises
P.O. Box 1300
Columbus, GA 31993
(404) 324-5617

Charglo

Indoor gas grill
Thermador/Waste King
5119 District Boulevard
Los Angeles, CA 90040

Charmglow

All sizes of outdoor gas grills, smoker, and accessories
Charmglow Products
P.O. Box 127
Bristol, WI 53104

Ducane

All sizes of outdoor gas grills
800 Dutch Square Boulevard
Columbia, SC 29210
(803) 798-1600

Durango Cooker

A gas boiler/cooker/grill
Durango Cookery
P.O. Box 2137
Durango, CO 81301
(303) 247-9511

Eurogrill

A portable fireplace and outdoor grill
Schoonmaker-Lynn Enterprises
4619 NW Barnes Road
Portland, OR 97210
(503) 222-5435

Fire Magic

Built-in outdoor charcoal or gas grills
Robert H. Peterson Company
530 N. Baldwin Park Boulevard
City of Industry, CA 91744

Hastybake

All sizes of outdoor charcoal grills
A division of C.B. Simmons, Inc.
P.O. Box 54645
Tulsa, OK 74155
(918) 665-8220

Happy Cooker

Charcoal and gas kettle grills and accessories
UNR Home Products
P.O. Box 429
Paris, IL 61944
(217) 465-5361

Hibachi

Portable grills
Barbecue Time, Inc.
P.O. Box 13637
Portland, OR 97213

Ichi

Portable electric or charcoal grill and fondue dish
The Ichi Corporation
7404 Trade Street
San Diego, CA 92121
(619) 695-9234

Imperial Kamado

Traditional kamado barbecue/smokers
Barbecues Galore
14048 East Firestone Boulevard
Santa Fe Springs, CA 90670
(714) 522-0660
(213) 921-7141

Jacuzzi

All sizes of gas grills and accessories
11511 New Benton Highway
P.O. Box 3533
Little Rock, AK 72203

Outdoor Chef

All types of barbecue parts and accessories
P.O. Box 534
Evansville, IN 47704-0534
(800) 862-7552

Paramount Housewares

Braziers
1035 Westminster Avenue
Alhambra, CA 91803
(213) 570-1601

Pyrobachi Oven

A portable charcoal grill/baker/griddle
Pyromid
302 West Evergreen
Redmond, OR 97756
(503) 548-1041

Sears/Kenmore

Outdoor charcoal and gas grills
See your local phone directory for the nearest Sears store.

Structo

Portables, braziers, covered charcoal and electric grills
King-Seeley Thermos Co.
Freeport, IL 61032
(815) 232-2111

The Texas Smoker

A large, Texas-shaped charcoal and wood smoker
Texas Designs
Harrell & Williams Co.
P.O. Box 171015
Arlington, TX 76003
(817) 265-4413

Turco

All sizes of gas grills
501 South Line Street
DuQuoin, IL 62832
(618) 542-4781

Weber

All sizes of charcoal and gas kettle grills and accessories
Weber-Stephen Products Company
200 East Daniels Road
Palatine, IL 60067
(800) 323-7598

TOOL SOURCES

Good-quality sturdy grill tools are not as easy to come by as might be expected. Stores that carry grills are the first place to look. We have also found that good hardware stores will more than likely have some of the key tools, such as tongs, mitts, and brushes. Many kitchenware stores are beginning to carry these tools, and you may also find them in restaurant supply stores. Many grill manufacturers sell a line of tools and grill accessories and may prove a useful resource. The following is a list of grill manufacturers who *do* carry tools, as well as a few mail-order tool outfits. For the addresses of the grill manufacturers, see page 103 under Grill Manufacturers.

Barbecues Galore

14048 East Firestone Boulevard
Santa Fe Springs, CA 90670
(714) 522-0660
(213) 921-7141

18922 Ventura Boulevard
Tarzana, CA 91356
(818) 435-7314

Charbroil

W.C. Bradley Enterprises
P.O. Box 1300
Columbus, GA 31993
(404) 324-5617

Charcoal Companion

Chimneys, tools
1025 Third Street
Oakland, CA 94607
(415) 893-3232

Charmglow

Charmglow Products
P.O. Box 127
Bristol, WI 53104

Happy Cooker

UNR Home Products
P.O. Box 429
Paris, IL 61944
(217) 465-5361

Jacuzzi

11511 New Benton Highway
P.O. Box 3533
Little Rock, AK 72203

Outdoor Chef

P.O. Box 534
Evansville, IN 47704-0534
(800) 862-7552

Sparta Brush Company

Basting brushes of all sizes
P.O. Box 317
Sparta, WI 54656

Sassafras Enterprises

Grill tools
East Bank Center
429 West Ohio Street
Chicago, IL 60610
(312) 670-5000

Christen, Inc.

Chimney Quick Charcoal Starter
59 Branch Street
St. Louis, MO 63147

Weber

Weber-Stephen Product Company
200 East Daniels Road
Palatine, IL 60067
(800) 323-7598

Grill shishkabob ingredients on separate skewers for even doneness

FUEL SOURCES

The following is a list of charcoal brands available in most grocery stores and hardware stores:

Chef Wood

Mesquite charcoal

Chef's Delight

Charcoal briquets

Del Sol

Mesquite charcoal

Kingsford

Briquets, briquets with mesquite wood, mesquite charcoal

Lazzari

Mesquite charcoal

Royal Oak

Mesquite and other hardwood charcoals, briquets

These charcoal and smoke chip distributors will also sell by mail-order or will direct you to their nearest distributors:

Charcoal Companion

California fruitwood chips
1025 Third Street
Oakland, CA 94607
(415) 893-3232

Country Picnic Foods

Mesquite wood, hickory chips
820 West Kearney
Mesquite, TX 75149
(214) 285-2345
(800) 527-4831

Humphrey Charcoal Corporation

Hardwood charcoal and 100%
hardwood charcoal briquets
P.O. Box 440
Brookville, PA 15825
(814) 849-2302

Lazzari Fuel Company

Mesquite charcoal from Mexico
P.O. Box 34051
San Francisco, CA 94034
(415) 467-2970
(800) 242-7265

Luhr Jensen & Sons

Hickory, alder, cherry, apple
smoking chips
P.O. Box 297
Hood River, OR 97031
(503) 386-3811

**Northcoast Valley Company/
Grapesmoke**

Grapevine cuttings
P.O. Box 1752
Santa Rosa, CA 95402
(707) 528-6252

Turkey Hill Farms

Apple, cherry, hickory, mesquite,
maple smoking chips
R.D. 1
P.O. Box 163
Red Hook, N.Y. 12571
(914) 756-2727

INDEX

Page numbers in **boldface** *type indicate recipes.*

BIBLIOGRAPHY

Campbell, Susan. *Cook's Tools*. New York: Bantam Books, 1980.

Cronin, Isaac; Harlow, Jay; and Johnson, Paul. *The California Seafood Cookbook*. Berkeley, CA: Aris Books, 1983.

The Editors of Sunset Books. *Barbecue Cookbook*. Menlo Park, CA: Lane Publishing Company, 1983.

The Editors of Time-Life Books. *Outdoor Cooking*. Alexandria, VA: Time-Life Books, 1983.

Ellis, Merle. *Cutting-up in the Kitchen*. San Francisco, CA.: Chronicle Books, 1975.

Hodgson, Moira. *The New York Times Gourmet Shopper*. New York: Times Books, 1983.

Root, Waverly, and de Rochemont, Richard. *Eating in America: A History*. New York: William Morrow & Company, 1976.

Sinnes, A. Cort, and Harlow, Jay. *The Grilling Book*. Berkeley, CA.: Aris Books, 1985.

Tannahill, Reay. *Food in History*. New York: Stein and Day, 1973.